Painting Landscapes

PAINTING LANDSCAPES

Harry R. Ballinger

Watson-Guptill Publications · New York

To Kay Mollison, my best friend and severest critic.

Contents

Introduction

With mixed emotions, I find myself starting another book on painting. I've always felt that a painter should stick to his painting and that if he had anything to say, his pictures should say it for him. It shouldn't be necessary for him to rush into print at the drop of a hat to explain his pictures or to explain how he feels about art in general. Writing should be left to the professional writers.

However, after the gratifying reception that my first two books received from the public, I decided that perhaps it was all right for an artist to break into print occasionally if he thought that his ideas and technical knowledge might benefit a wider audience.

HOW THIS BOOK CAME ABOUT

When I started studying art years ago, I was fortunate in having fine instruction from a number of first-rate artists. They were unselfish, dedicated men who enjoyed helping their students to get the right start on their artistic careers. I'll never forget their help or cease to be grateful. That was when I learned many of the painting ideas that I've used ever since.

The way I can show my appreciation for all the help that I've received during my life is to pass my knowledge of painting on to others through teaching and by writing books. It does make an artist feel good to know that he's been able to help others paint better pictures.

When I wrote *Painting Surf and Sea,* I received letters from as far away as New Zealand. With the publication of *Painting Boats and Harbors,* there was an equally gratifying response from all over America. I've greatly appreciated the wonderful letters from so many nice people, telling me how much they liked my books and how helpful these books had been in solving readers' own painting problems. A great many letter writers asked me when I was going to write another book, preferably one on landscape painting.

After considerable thought on the subject—plus some judicious prodding from my esteemed publishers and my Gentle Wife—I've finally decided to write the kind of book on landscape painting that I would like to have found when I first started to paint the great outdoors.

REALISTIC AND ABSTRACT PAINTING

My own work is in the traditional realistic style, so my instructions in this book will be based on a realistic approach to nature.

At present, there is a great deal of painting around the country in the modern style. This work ranges from semi-abstracts, which look a little like the subjects they portray, to really way-out abstract expressionist paintings, which seem to take right off for the stratosphere.

I think there is a lot of very fine semi-abstract work that is creative and inspiring to look at. The modernists, with their imaginative approach to design and color, have had a good effect on the art world. I greatly doubt that abstract painting will entirely replace representational pictures in the future, but I think that the modernists have been a good influence on traditional art; we will never again go back to the old dry-as-dust chromos of an earlier period.

I always enjoy seeing the big modern shows and I think that everyone can learn a lot from them.

A BRIEF SUMMARY OF THIS BOOK

I believe you'll find this book simply written, with clear explanations of all the problems involved in landscape painting, from the fundamentals of technique to the more sophisticated problems of mood and feeling.

I remarked before that I'd rather look at pictures than wade through a lot of words. So this book will have lots of large pictures and diagrams to further explain the text. Perhaps after one reading, you can skip the text completely and just look at the pictures.

In this book there will be chapters on painting materials; color mixing; composition; and selecting the subject to paint. You will find step-by-step painting demonstrations, showing the development of painting from the rough lay-in to the finished picture.

There will be descriptions of outdoor painting on location and indoor painting from sketches; special instructions for painting skies, water, trees, rocks, snow, and buildings; guidance on painting rural scenes, towns and cities, landscapes in the four seasons, atmospheric effects, moonlight, sunsets, fog, etc., and recommendations for painting pictures in limited and arbitrary color schemes.

Finally, there are ten landscape drawings that can be used as material for practice paintings of your own.

Of course, the book will be profusely illustrated with many large paintings and drawings for those who would rather look than read.

PLEASURES AND PROBLEMS OF LANDSCAPE PAINTING

I've often been asked what makes a good subject for landscape painting. I think any scene that awakens your interest on your first glance would be worth trying to paint. Perhaps it's the color scheme that appeals to you, the black-and-white composition (distribution of light and shade), some special mood, atmospheric effect, or unusual subject matter. You have to be attracted to the scene in order to paint an interesting picture.

Aside from the difficulty of trying to capture on canvas the scene in front of you, a landscape painter has to overcome all kinds of other problems. There are the problems of the changing weather; the interested spectators who breathe down the back of your neck and ask the silliest questions; the unfriendly landowners who claim that you're trespassing; the friendly cows who think your palette is a new and fascinating kind of *hors d'oeuvre* and who would just love to make a banquet out of your discarded paint rags.

There are also unfriendly policemen who claim you're obstructing traffic by causing a crowd of interested spectators to collect around you.

However, there are so many people painting outside these days that it isn't much of a novelty to see an artist at work any more; usually you're not bothered at all.

In spite of all these minor hazards, you're painting the grandest subject in the world: the great outdoors. When you succeed in painting a good landscape, it's worth all the trouble and grief you have to go through. So here's more power to you, with my hope that this book will help you overcome at least *some* of the technical problems that you will encounter when painting landscapes.

HARRY R. BALLINGER

9

1. Materials and Equipment

There has always been some difference of opinion among students as to the amount and kind of equipment necessary for outdoor painting.

One nice gal who used to study with me at Rockport, Massachusetts every summer, used to carry her paints and brushes in an old shoe box and didn't have any easel at all. She used to arrive with a car and chauffeur every day, so it couldn't have been lack of funds that was responsible for her scanty painting equipment.

On the other hand, when I was first studying art out in San Francisco, there was a young Italian in the class who had hardly a cent to his name, but used the finest paints and brushes and the best linen canvas. I asked him one time why he wanted to use such expensive canvas for his practice work. He said, "You never know when comes the masterpiece." He was certainly well prepared and I hope the masterpieces all came along on schedule.

Good equipment doesn't necessarily produce a good picture—but it helps.

For the benefit of those who have had no previous experience with painting in oils, I'll list the equipment needed for outdoor painting.

SKETCH BOX AND PALETTE

You will need a sketch box to carry your brushes, paints, and other equipment. A 12 × 16 box is a good size, though I use a 16 × 20 box because I like a little more room for everything. Sketch boxes are usually made of wood, though some people prefer an aluminum box because of its lighter weight.

A wooden palette usually comes with the sketch box, but you may use a paper palette with disposable tear-off sheets if it is more convenient. If you use a wooden palette, it's a good idea to rub a little linseed oil on it when new, in order to give the palette a smoother and less porous surface on which to mix your paint.

Don't buy a fitted box, which comes with all materials and equipment pre-selected for you. It contains a lot of useless colors and is much too expensive. It's better to select your own colors and buy only the ones that you really need.

EASEL AND STOOL

You'll want a good solid sketching easel, either wood or aluminum. My favorite is the Anderson easel (sometimes called the Gloucester easel) which is manufactured by Edith Anderson Miller in Cincinnati, Ohio.

This portable unit combines easel and paint box.

This type of easel has a shelf-like arrangement below the canvas for holding the sketch box and palette. This easel folds up compactly and has a shoulder strap for carrying: a great help when you are crawling over stone walls and barbed-wire fences with a sketch box in one hand and two canvases in the other.

If you decide on an aluminum easel, get one that has a place to rest your palette, as it's extremely inconvenient to hold your palette in your left hand. It's better to have your left hand free to hold a paint rag and extra brushes. If your easel hasn't a place for your palette, you can nail

This folding easel has a pull-out drawer arrangement for your materials.

Start out with eight brushes in pairs of roughly equal size.

three stretcher sticks together to form a platform on which to rest your palette.

There is one other type of easel, called a French easel, which has the advantage of combining the sketch box with the easel itself. When the easel is opened up for use, the sketch box makes a handy spot on which to rest the palette and other equipment.

The French easel isn't quite so strongly constructed as the Anderson easel and it's quite expensive. But it's a great advantage to have only one object to carry on your sketching trip. For those who prefer to paint sitting down, any strong, light folding stool will be satisfactory.

BRUSHES AND PALETTE KNIFE

You should have at least six brushes, ranging in width from a quarter of an inch to an inch. They should be flat with a square end. I prefer bristle brushes to the softer sables; you're liable to get your picture too polished and slick-looking with sable brushes.

It's a good idea to have two brushes of approximately the same size: one for light color and one for dark. For your smaller brushes, perhaps you might have sizes 2 and 3; for the next size, 4 and 5; and for the larger sizes, 7 and 8. You can get still larger sizes if you are painting larger canvases. For fine lines you may get a number 1 brush; but you

Hold the brush well back from the bristles.

You can also paint with a palette knife.

Laid out clockwise, starting at the lower left hand corner, my palette consists of (A) ultramarine blue deep; (B) cerulean blue; (C) viridian, occasionally; (D) zinc white; (E) cadmium yellow pale; (F) cadmium orange; (G) cadmium red light; (H) cadmium red deep; (I) alizarin crimson, occasionally.

can make a fine line by using the side of your larger brushes, thus you will seldom need a small brush. It is always better to use as large a brush as possible, in order to cover your canvas rapidly and to keep your picture broad and simple.

For mixing paint, painting, and scraping, you'll need a palette knife. This should be the trowel-like type, with the blade surface a little below the handle. This shape is easier to use than the straight type and you get less paint on your hands.

MEDIUM AND TURPENTINE

Medium is the liquid that you mix with your paint when you apply the paint to your canvas. I use a mixture of linseed oil and turpentine, half and half. Any good brand of clear gum turpentine from a paint store is all right; but the oil must be a purified linseed oil, obtainable only at an artists' material shop.

You will need an oil cup two inches in width to hold medium while you paint. Buy two bottles that will fit into your sketch box: one to hold your medium, the other for turpentine to clean your palette and brushes. I don't clean my brushes with turpentine while painting; just dipping

15

Cut a view finder out of cardboard.

them lightly in my oil cup, then wiping them with my paint rag seems to clean them sufficiently for me to go on painting.

ARTISTS' COLORS

For many years, I have used a standard high-key palette that has become known as the "Ballinger Palette." I didn't originate it, but I have found over the years that it works very well for almost any kind of painting. My colors consist of ultramarine blue; cerulean blue; zinc white; cadmium yellow pale; cadmium orange; cadmium red light; cadmium red deep; and alizarin crimson. You may also buy burnt sienna and yellow ochre, if you wish, but you will have only occasional use for them.

16

VARNISH

You will also need retouching varnish. This is a light, quick-drying varnish that will restore the gloss to any portion of your picture that has dried in. You can buy this in handy spray cans or you can buy it in bottles and spray the varnish on with a fixative blower. If the canvas is quite dry, you can use a soft, clean brush or rag to apply the varnish to the picture.

VIEW FINDER

Another useful piece of equipment is the view finder. This is simply a piece of cardboard with a rectangular opening for viewing the scene. The cardboard has a border wide enough to blank out all but the scene you want to paint. When you are sketching outdoors, there is so much to see that it is hard to concentrate on any particular portion of the scene. The view finder helps you decide what to include in your picture and what to leave out.

CANVAS AND CANVAS PANELS

The last item to consider is what to paint on. Canvas mounted on a cardboard panel is good, as panels take up very little room and can be easily transported. If you are using panels the size of your sketch box, you can carry them in the lid of your box. The lid has grooves into which your panels can easily slide.

For sizes larger than 16 × 20, I would suggest a stretched canvas: cotton or linen, tacked to a wooden frame.

Some artists paint on Masonite or wooden panels. Wooden panels have been used for generations and have a handsome surface to paint on. The only objection to their use is that it's hard to get the right kind of well-seasoned wood that won't warp or split.

Before you use wood panels, they have to be treated with a preparation of gesso or white lead. This also applies to Masonite. While Masonite is easy to get in any lumber yard, I don't like the surface; one side is too smooth and the other too rough. However, it will probably last forever, if that's any comfort.

CLEANING YOUR PALETTE AND BRUSHES

When you've finished the day's work, it's a good idea to empty the remaining medium in the oil cup onto the palette and use the medium to clean off the center of the palette, leaving the gobs of tube color around the edges. This color will usually stay moist for several days, so it won't be wasted.

If you're using a disposable paper palette, you can transfer the piles of paint to a fresh sheet and throw away the old one.

When you finish the day's painting, you can place the brushes in a flat tin of kerosene, with the handles resting on the edge of the pan and the bristles lying flat on the bottom of the pan. This is much better for the brushes than to stand them upright in kerosene; the pressure on the bristles is liable to bend and distort them. When you wish to use the brushes again, just wipe them off with a rag and they'll be ready for work.

I wouldn't let brushes stand in turpentine; it makes them gummy. However, you can clean them all right if you just dip the brushes in turpentine and then wipe them with your paint rag. Every two or three weeks, you can give brushes a real bath with brown laundry soap and water, taking care to rub the soap right up to the ferrule of the brush, so that no paint will harden in the bristles to spoil them. Your brushes will last longer if they are not washed too often, as constant washing wears them out. It also wears the artist out, which is something to be avoided at all costs.

To keep brushes soft and clean between painting sessions, I leave them in a tray of kerosene, resting on newspaper in case of spills.

18

2. Composition

Practically all artists who paint in a simple, direct manner realize that it's necessary to organize the main areas of the picture into simple masses of light and shade. A broad method of composing or painting depends on a broad conception of a scene.

PLANNING THE BLACK-AND-WHITE DESIGN

Whenever I look at a picture, I always try to see it as a simple, two-toned pattern of light and dark, with everything in the picture forming part of either the light design or the dark design. While color is unquestionably important in a picture and adds greatly to its visual appeal, I believe that a well-arranged pattern of light and dark is absolutely necessary to produce a good picture. It is the foundation and the framework on which you construct the entire painting.

When you are planning the black-and-white design of the picture, it's a good idea to tie the dark areas together; have one dark spot blend into or overlap an adjoining dark area to form a large, irregular shape, rather than a number of isolated spots. The light spots should be tied up in the same manner.

This simple, two-toned, poster-like arrangement will determine the big over-all design of your picture. This basic design can be modified as you go along by adding varieties of tone in your light and dark areas and by adding details where they are necessary. The nearer you can come to preserving your original big, simple pattern in the finished picture, the better the picture will be.

In a landscape, it's easy to see a two-toned pattern of light and dark. Very often your sky will be part of your light pattern, with white buildings and the light parts of your foreground. The darks will be trees, grass, mountains, any shadows, and dark-toned buildings.

ADIRONDACK FARM   When you are studying a scene that you wish to paint, try to see it as a simple two-toned pattern of light and dark. Everything in the picture will be part of either your dark or light pattern. In this Adirondack scene, it is easy, if you look at the picture through half-closed eyes, to see which parts of the picture are part of the dark pattern, and which are part of the light. Collection, Mr. and Mrs. William B. Andrus.

Before I describe some of the more popular types of composition used in the structural designs of most pictures, I would like to explain what is meant by balance in a picture.

Pictures are composed on the principle of the steel-yard balance. If this term is confusing, think of the old idea of the see-saw. An adult has to sit well in toward the center of the see-saw to be balanced by a child sitting out on the opposite end. Apply this principle to a picture: a large light or dark spot near the center of the picture can be balanced by a smaller spot out near the edge.

POPULAR TYPES OF COMPOSITION

Some of the more popular types of composition, used by artists for centuries, are:

1 First, there's the picture which is predominantly light, with balanced dark spots. The picture of the old shack and dead tree (page 25) is balanced by the dark figure and grass near the edge of the composition.

2 The same composition in reverse is equally good, as shown on page 26 in the night scene of the white house with the light path leading to it.

3 A picture with a dark base and a light upper part is effective. The dark base gives strength and stability to the design. The picture of the old farm at twilight (page 27) illustrates this composition.

4 The same composition in reverse is shown in the snow scene with the dark evening sky (page 28).

5 A pyramid, with the weight and interest building up toward the center, is always strong and effective. The mountain picture on page 29 illustrates this type of arrangement.

6 There is also the L-shaped picture, which builds up along one side of the painting. This was a favorite of the old masters. I don't know what the Barbizon School of French landscape painters would have done without this idea. The picture of the valley view on page 30 represents this type of arrangement.

TWO DRAWINGS The two drawings, I hope, will show how to tie together the dark spots in a picture to produce one large pattern of dark. This can be done by having one dark area overlap an adjoining one. This produces one large dark pattern instead of a number of isolated spots of dark. You do the same with your light spots. This simplifies your pattern of light and shade and makes the design of your picture more easily understood from a distance. It's absolutely necessary to tie up the spots of light and dark in your picture in order to produce a decorative and professional looking painting. Some of the primitive painters are the only ones who fail to make use of this extremely logical and decorative plan of composing a picture.

7 The S-shaped composition—in which the interest swings through the picture from top to bottom like the letter *S*—is one of the most useful forms in designing a landscape. I often use this device, sometimes in combination with some of the other standard compositions. The picture of the winding stream on page 31 is an example of this type of composition.

8 Sometimes the picture can be constructed of alternating horizontal bands of light and dark. The spring landscape on page 32 is an example of this arrangement.

9 A circular design is good, as it keeps the eye in the picture and concentrates attention on the central part of the composition. This same composition is sometimes called the "tunnel," because it depends on the receding perspective lines and receding values to carry your eye deep into the picture to an opening at the end of the "tunnel" and a possible center of interest. The tree-shaded road with distant cabin (page 33) is this type of picture.

10 A composition of radiating or converging lines calls attention to the center of interest by leading your glance to the focal point of the lines. The painting of trees by the river (page 34), with the lines of the clouds leading to the center of interest, illustrates this composition.

22

WOODED HILL TOP   Here is an example of the steel-yard principle: the large darks of the trees near the center are balanced by the smaller tree at the left-hand edge of the painting.

11 The final compositional idea is the pattern, which consists of a decorative arrangement of the light and dark areas to form an interesting design throughout the picture. A great many pictures are constructed on this basis. The Vermont picture on page 35 is an example of this kind of picture.

Very often a combination of several of these compositional ideas can be used in the same picture.

If you succeed in getting a fine decorative arrangement of your black-and-white pattern, you'll have a good picture. On the other hand, if the composition doesn't work out well, you might just as well give up the whole project and start another picture from a different angle.

One way of learning more about composition is to study every fine picture that you see and try to decide what kind of composition was used in its construction. By studying other paintings, you can see how the principles of design and balance can be applied to your own pictures.

COMPOSITION I: WHERE THE HEART IS   One popular type of composition is a light picture with balanced spots of dark. The dark mass of the shack and trees near the center of the canvas is balanced by the figure out near the edge on the opposite side.

COMPOSITION II: NIGHT SCENE, WHITE HOUSE   A dark picture with balanced light spots: the first composition in reverse is also effective. The moonlight picture of the white house is balanced by the light road on the other side.

COMPOSITION III: SNOW SCENE, DARK EVENING SKY A picture with a light base and dark upper part is effective. This is a composition that is often seen at sunset or twilight.

COMPOSITION IV: OLD FARM AT TWILIGHT   The same pattern in reverse is also good. The winter scene at night shows this type of arrangement.

COMPOSITION V: MT. CLEMENTS   A pyramid with the weight and interest building up toward the center makes a strong and effective arrangement. Most portraits have this type of composition with the lines all leading up the center of the picture to the center of interest, the head.

29

COMPOSITION VI: VALLEY VIEWS This is the L-shaped picture with the weight and interest building up one side of the composition. Just about every other landscape of the old-time painters used this type of composition.

COMPOSITION VII: WINDING STREAM The S-shaped composition in which the interest swings through the picture from top to bottom like the letter S. This line of interest can be used in combination with other standard types of composition. I believe that I use it in a lot of my own pictures.

COMPOSITION VIII: SPRING LANDSCAPE Sometimes the picture can be constructed with alternating bands of light and dark. The composition is nice for prairies or marsh scenes.

COMPOSITION IX: THE CLEARING   This is a circular design or tunnel. The eye is carried by the receding perspective lines into the opening at the end of the tunnel, an area which is probably the center of interest.

COMPOSITION X: TREES BY RIVER A composition with radiating or converging lines leads your eye into the center of interest. The receding lines of the bank of the river lead your eye to the trees in the center. The line of the clouds also points toward the center of interest.

COMPOSITION XI: BELVEDERE CENTER   This type of composition is called the pattern and consists of a decorative arrangement of the light and dark areas to form an interesting design throughout the picture. This idea can be used in combination with almost any of the other kinds of composition.

3. Simplified Perspective

It isn't necessary for a landscape painter to know as much about perspective as an architect, but there are a few general principles that the painter should understand in order to paint a good landscape.

There are two kinds of perspective: linear and aerial. Linear perspective concerns itself with the receding lines of all objects in a picture as these lines move back to the horizon line. Aerial perspective concerns itself with the effect of atmosphere on color and values (darkness or lightness) as objects recede into the distance.

LINEAR PERSPECTIVE

In linear perspective, the receding lines of all objects in a picture converge at a point on the horizon line, at the level of your eye. Your eye level determines the horizon line, since the eye line and the horizon line are the same.

The receding lines of objects *above* your eye level come *down* to the horizon. All receding lines *below* your eye level go *up* to the horizon. A man standing on a hill would see a high horizon line on a level with his eye. A man on flat ground would see a lower horizon. If you're painting high hills or mountains, a low horizon line will make the hills look higher. On the other hand, if you're on a high elevation and the view that you're painting is more or less panoramic, the horizon should be placed near the top of the canvas. In this case, the receding lines of most objects below you in the picture would go *up* to the horizon line.

PLACING THE HORIZON LINE

In most outdoor views, the painter can arbitrarily place his horizon line anywhere he wishes; he can merely assume that he is at that elevation. If you're painting street scenes, it's advisable to use a horizon line at the eye line of a person standing in the street. If you're thinking of putting figures on a level street, you must remember that the eye line of all figures, no matter how far back in the picture, would be at the same level.

NEW ENGLAND TOWN This picture, of a little New England town by a river, has a high horizon line. Most of the buildings are below your eye level, so their receding lines go up to a vanishing point somewhere on the horizon line.

Horizon

Horizon

THE GOOD EARTH This is a picture with a low horizon line or eye-line. The interest has been concentrated on the sky, with the ground, trees, and houses of rather secondary interest. When you paint a mountain scene, a low horizon makes the mountains seem larger and more impressive.

THE HARBOR AT PORT CLYDE In this view of the harbor at Port Clyde, I was up on a hill, and the view is more or less panoramic. So of course I used a fairly high horizon line. The receding lines of the wharves and buildings all went up to vanishing points on the horizon line.

Horizon

Aerial perspective simply means that all colors and values of objects become paler and grayer as the objects recede toward the horizon. There is almost always a certain amount of water vapor or dust in the air, which causes distant objects to be seen through a kind of haze. The result is that your light spots are a little darker in the distance and your dark spots a little grayer.

Naturally, the greater the space between an artist and an object the more air will be present in that space. To the painter, the color of the air is the color of the sky. Thus, the distance of an object from the viewer can be suggested by the amount of *sky color* that the painter mixes with the *local color* of the object. This addition of sky color produces the effect of atmosphere and allows the different portions of the picture to appear at the right distance from the viewer.

You can see the effect of the atmosphere on a summer landscape, where the green trees take on a bluer and grayer color as they recede into the distance. This effect is also noticeable in an autumn landscape, where the warm red foliage on a nearby hillside takes on a cooler, more purplish appearance the farther away this foliage stands in the picture.

PERSPECTIVE AND DETAIL

By painting the foreground with brighter color and stronger lights and darks, you have the opportunity to gray your color and values as you go back into the picture. Sometimes it helps the effect of aerial perspective in your picture to pile paint in the foreground, suggesting form and detail, then paint the distant areas more thinly. Many painters have used this idea with great success.

Aerial perspective also influences the amount of *detail* that you see in receding objects. A tree a mile away isn't an object made up of leaves and branches, but a solid colored mass, having a pattern of light and shade, and perhaps perforated by the sky.

In other words an artist doesn't try to paint nature the way it actually is—leaf by leaf, stone by stone—but the way it looks to the eye.

LEARNING MORE ABOUT PERSPECTIVE

If you wish to learn more about perspective you can find a number of excellent books on the subject at almost any library. Ernest Watson's

WESTERN TOWN   Here we have a sketch of some people on a level street with the eye-line that of the standing figure. You will notice that the eyes of all the figures, no matter how distant, are practically on the same level.

Horizon

41

SPRING FLOOD This Vermont scene near Jay Peak was painted in the early spring. The river had overflowed its banks but was fairly well behaved at that moment. All distant objects were grayed-up by the hazy atmosphere. There is very little detail to be seen in the distant woods and hills. The strongest darks are in the foreground and center of interest.

THE BRIDGE   I tried to dramatize the last voyage of a fine old ship being towed to her final resting place. The Brooklyn Bridge has been painted many times, but always looks impressive in a picture. Its sweeping lines make an interesting contrast with the distant sky-line of Manhattan. Courtesy, The Kennedy Galleries.

Perspective For Sketchers and *How To Use Creative Perspective* are good basic books.

I believe that there is a saying to the effect that too much learning maketh a man mad. I imagine that whoever coined that was thinking of someone trying to learn all about perspective. You could spend the rest of your life studying the subject and if you didn't end up mad, I think you would be a good candidate, at least, for psychiatric attention.

Vanishing Point

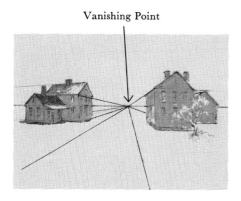

4. Color and Values

Color plays a vitally important part in all pictures and must be as carefully organized as the black-and-white composition of your painting. There are a few basic facts about color that should be understood before starting to paint a picture.

WARM AND COOL COLORS

First, think of color as being either warm or cool. The warm colors are red, yellow, orange, reddish greens, reddish purples, and browns and grays in which the warm colors predominate. The cool colors are the blues, blue-greens, blue-purples, and all the bluish grays.

In a fall or winter landscape, the ground, grass, bushes, and wooded hillsides will all be warm in color, especially if there is any sunlight. The only cool color will be the blue of the sky; its *down-light* on the tops of trees and bushes; and the shadows on the ground that are exposed to the cool light from the sky. Distant hills or mountains will also be on the cool side, because when they are seen through the intervening atmosphere they take on more of the cool color of the sky.

PRIMARY AND SECONDARY COLORS

The next thing to remember is the spectrum theory of color, which breaks color up into its primary parts: red, yellow, and blue. Then, mixing equal parts of the two primaries, we get the secondaries: orange, green, and purple.

The secondaries are complementary to the primary colors. Orange is complementary to blue; green to red; and purple to yellow. A glance at the color wheel on page 57 will show you that the colors directly across the circle from each other are complementaries.

COLOR SCHEMES

With the color wheel as a guide, there are a number of color harmonies you can use in a picture:

1   Monochromatic color means using just one color in different shades and values.

2   Complementary harmony is achieved by using colors directly opposite each other on the color circle.

3   Analogous harmony is composed of colors close together on the color wheel; in other words, any small section of the color wheel.

4   A split complementary scheme uses colors closely related to one or both complements. This is a combination of complementary and analogous schemes: an extremely useful color harmony in many pictures.

KEEP YOUR COLORS SIMPLE

When they start out with a sketch box full of lovely colors, most beginners want to use all of them in each picture that they paint. Their idea is that if *one* bright color looks good, a lot of colors will look much better. This isn't the case at all. You'll find that a picture painted with one or two colors is much more harmonious and striking than one done with a more complicated color scheme.

A painting with one color predominating, and its complementary used more sparingly, can be immensely effective. I've often painted a picture that was composed of different tones of reddish brown, with a few touches of green. The effect is so good that you'd swear that there were at least a half-dozen colors used in the picture.

COLORS ON THE PALETTE

The choice of colors that comprise an artist's palette is a very personal thing, and there are as many ideas on the subject as there are artists. Some like a lot of earth colors—burnt sienna, Indian red, yellow ochre, olive-green, black, to name a few—while others prefer a more high-keyed palette.

It's so easy to get a lot of mud color in a picture that I prefer to start, at least, with some nice clean color, even though the finished picture doesn't always live up to its colorful start.

46

THE WHARF AT PORT CLYDE This view of the wharf at Port Clyde was painted in a limited color scheme in tones of brown with just a few touches of dull green.

I use comparatively few colors, as I believe that you can get more sparkle and freshness by mixing two colors to make a third than by using a corresponding color right out of the tube. My palette—which has been called the "Ballinger Palette," as I mentioned earlier—is simply the standard high-keyed palette, with no greens, purple, black, or earth colors. For almost any kind of picture, I find this palette quite ideal and I use it for most of my painting. The colors should be arranged on your palette starting with the cool ones on the left, then the white, followed by the warm ones arranged in the order of the color wheel.

1 Ultramarine blue. This is a dark, purplish blue. Combined with red, it can be used for strong darks. I use the blue to darken the color, then add cadmium red deep and cadmium red light or orange, depending upon how warm I want the dark to be. The darks should be kept a little on the warm side to give them more richness and depth, rather than having the darks a cold blue or purple.

2 Cerulean blue. This is a paler, more greenish blue, and makes lovely, pearly grays when mixed with cadmium red light and white. If you wish more of a tan color, add a little cadmium orange to the gray mixture. However, don't add cadmium yellow pale; this will produce a greenish tint. Cerulean blue is a very useful color because it is already slightly grayed as it comes from the tube; thus, it can be used to gray other colors or combinations of colors. Cerulean blue also makes some fine greens when combined with cadmium yellow pale.

3 Thalo blue or viridian. Once in a while, you can use some thalo blue or viridian in some special spot, but I don't think that you'll use either of them very often. Thalo blue is a powerful dye, like Prussian blue, and should be used very sparingly. When mixed with white, thalo blue will make a strong, light blue that can be used in painting a sky. For ordinary use, thalo blue is too powerful for the other colors on your palette. Viridian is a cool blue-green that is very effective when used in a picture with tones of orangy red.

4 Zinc white. Be sure that you buy a brand that is fairly liquid so that it will mix readily with your colors and flow on easily. You'll use white to gray up your colors when you are mixing light hues; but don't mix

GHOST TOWN   The small ghost town of Ashcroft, Colorado, was painted with only a couple of colors: a purplish brown and a pale yellow.

too much white with your color, because you're liable to give a chalky look to your painting. For instance, you can get a light-enough green by mixing cadmium yellow pale with your cerulean blue without using any white at all.

5 *Cadmium yellow pale* is like a lemon yellow or chrome yellow. Be sure that the art materials dealer doesn't sell you cadmium yellow light; this is a much warmer yellow and doesn't work as well as cadmium yellow pale.

6 *Cadmium orange* is the warmest kind of yellow. By mixing cadmium yellow pale and cadmium orange, you can get any degree of warmth you wish in your yellows.

7 *Cadmium red light*. Be sure that it is an orangy red like vermilion.

8 *Cadmium red deep or medium*. Either of these colors is all right for your dark reds, or combined with ultramarine blue to make black.

9 *Alizarin crimson* is preferable to rose madder because the alizarin is a more permanent color. I use alizarin crimson only occasionally in a picture. When combined with blues, it makes a rip-roaring purple, a color that can be left out of most color schemes, I think. However, when mixed with white, alizarin crimson makes some lovely, delicate pinks. When used with cadmium red light, it makes a strong and brilliant red.

MIXING COLORS

Here, in brief, is the way to mix some of the colors you'll use most often.

Black. Ultramarine blue and cadmium red deep, with just a touch of cadmium orange, will give the effect of black, though it will have more brilliance than black paint.

Darks. For dark reds or browns, use ultramarine blue with cadmium red deep or cadmium red light. For browns, use a little orange with the cadmium red light, and less of the ultramarine blue. For lighter browns, use cerulean mixed with a cadmium red light or cadmium orange.

MT. WASHINGTON   This view of Mt. Washington, New Hampshire, was painted in early spring. The small stream was still frozen over, but no other snow was visible except on the mountain itself. It is a warm picture. The distant hill, the trees, and darker bushes are a reddish brown. The sky and field are tan; the evergreen trees a warm dull green. The only cool spots are located in parts of the sky and in shadows on the snow at the mountain top. These were not a strong blue, but more of a lavender blue.

51

THEDE'S PLACE   The picture of the house on Cotton Hill was painted in tones of dull orange tan and a warm green. The distant hill was purple; the sky and field were in shades of tan.

MOUNTAIN PASS   The Rockies in winter are wonderful to paint. This picture is an example of the whole value range from light to dark.

White. Use zinc white, of course, but you'll generally add just a touch of warm or cool color, because the whites you see in nature are seldom exactly white.

Grays. Mix cerulean blue and cadmium red light with white.

Tan. Add a little cadmium orange to the above gray mixture.

Greens. For light greens, use cerulean blue and cadmium yellow pale. For darker greens, use ultramarine blue instead of cerulean. If you want a dark olive-green, use ultramarine blue combined with cadmium orange.

When you're mixing a color, try not to mix the paint too thoroughly on the palette. You'll have more color vibration on the canvas if your paint isn't over-blended. You'll get an effect of broken color which will give a sparkle to the picture. Many artists will mix up a big pile of paint with a palette knife before applying the paint to the canvas. This may save a little time, but I think you'll get a fresher effect on your canvas if you just partially mix the paint on your palette with your brush, then let the final mixing occur when you apply the paint to your picture.

VALUES

By values, we mean the degree of lightness or darkness of any particular part of a picture of any color. Value also means the degree of lightness or darkness of one color compared to another. Tone means roughly the same as value. Halftones are the values in a picture that are neither light nor dark, but lie between the light and dark masses.

Key means the over-all color value of a picture. A high-keyed painting will be one with light, bright color, and probably no very *dark* darks. A low-keyed picture will have dark, somber colors. The color range might start from almost black, and the lightest values might be nowhere near a real white.

As I explained in the chapter on composition, the light-and-dark pattern of the picture is the framework on which the whole painting is constructed. Without the right values or tonality a picture just falls apart.

Proper tonality not only enhances the color in a picture, but has a decided charm of its own. We've all seen black-and-white reproductions

FISH-HOUSES AT PORT CLYDE I tried merely to suggest the clutter of gear and boats that you see around fishing shacks. The figures are very roughly indicated, because I wanted them to be of incidental interest in the picture. This scene was painted in only two colors: a reddish brown and a warm green. I find that a picture painted in a limited color scheme often looks more striking than one painted in a number of colors. I used a pyramid composition in this picture.

that were a lot more attractive than the original pictures. This is due to the tonal harmony of the picture and to the charm of its light-and-dark design.

VALUE RANGE

The values in a picture range from light to dark, with as many variations in between as you wish. However, it's better to use a few values instead of a great many; a picture with three or four main values has more strength and simplicity.

Generally, the nature of the picture will dictate how much of the entire range of possible tones, from light to dark, will be used. Almost any picture—if it doesn't have very much atmosphere—may have the entire tonal range from light to dark, with strong contrasts, accents, and highlights. However, it's often necessary to limit the values in your picture to the light end, the dark end, or the middle register.

Nature usually furnishes suggestions for the tonal scale to be used. For instance, a high-key picture of a hazy spring landscape, with no very strong darks, would undoubtedly call for a key near the light end of your value scale. A foggy day, with no strong lights or darks, would be in the middle register. A moonlight scene would be in the darker portion of the tonal range.

When you have your light and dark values approximately established, you'll find that it's easy to work out the remaining tones throughout the picture. When you're planning your dark masses, remember to keep them grayed just a little, so that you'll have darker pigment to use as accents in the dark areas, as well as throughout the entire picture. The lights should also be modified (grayed) a little to allow you to use a stronger light for highlights wherever needed.

Generally, your strongest lights and darkest darks will be in your foreground or at the center of interest, with distant parts of the picture kept grayer due to the influence of the atmosphere on color and values.

It will help you to determine the values in a picture if you pick out the lightest lights and the darkest darks, then compare all other tones to them to get the proper values.

To see the simple light-and-dark pattern of a view, it helps to half close your eyes and squint at the scene. This simplifies all the details in both your light areas and your dark masses.

Color wheel

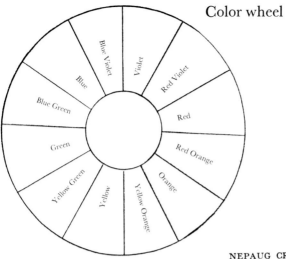

NEPAUG CREEK   This painting of the creek
is in the darker end of the value scale.

ONE MORE WINTER This is a picture with side lighting. The low sunlight from the right side of the picture hits more strongly on some of the upright spots of snow, making them appear lighter than the more horizontal planes of snow. The apple tree in the foreground had blown over but was still alive and no doubt would produce its usual crop of apples and worms next summer. Collection, Dr. John Houlihan.

5. Planning the Picture

When you're starting out on a painting trip, be sure that you have all your equipment with you. There's nothing more depressing than arriving somewhere on location and discovering that something vital—like white paint or canvas—has been left behind. I remember one year I got all the way up to the top of Vermont before I discovered that I had left my easel behind!

If you travel by car, you can carry enough equipment around with you to stock an art-supply store but you have to be more selective if you travel on foot. Be sure that you have your paint box, brushes, paints, canvas, and easel with you. Also have a sketchbook and view finder to help you decide on the exact composition that you want to paint.

SELECTING YOUR SUBJECT

When you get out on location, it's a good idea to look the scene over carefully and select a view that interests you. If it appeals to you and you think it might make a good picture, paint it. Don't waste time trying to find something better; you may not find it. Don't make the mistake of selecting too complicated a subject. A fine picture can be made from two or three large trees, perhaps a mountain, with some foreground objects or some old shacks in a field. In most scenes that you find there is material for a number of pictures. When you decide on the portion of the scene that you want to paint, look at it from several different directions to be sure that you have an angle that will give you the most pleasing arrangement of the lights and darks. At this point, it sometimes helps to look at the scene through a view finder as described on page 17. In outdoor sketching there is so much to see that it's often hard to decide just what to include in your picture and what to leave out. The view finder will help you decide exactly how much of the scene to paint.

MARSH'S POND   This autumn view of Marsh's Pond has the light hitting the picture from the left-hand side. The trees across the pond were a riot of orange, yellows, and reds. The clump of grass in the right foreground was a dark wine-red. The reeds along the water's edge were a pale yellow.

LANE'S COVE This picture was painted with a back lighting. The upright planes are in shadow, while the light falls on the top horizontal planes of the different objects in the picture.

PRELIMINARY PENCIL SKETCHES

Before starting your picture, it's a good idea to make one or two pencil sketches to be sure that you have a good black-and-white pattern for your picture. Then, carefully note the direction of the light and which way the sun is moving, so that the light effect in your painting won't change too drastically. You can usually guess approximately where your shadows will be in about an hour; then you can make allowances for that much of a change in the direction of the light.

LIGHTING

The painting will generally have a simpler pattern of light and dark if you can use a sidelight or a backlight from within the picture. In a scene with back lighting, all your upright planes are in shadow, while the light hits on the tops of objects and on the horizontal planes.

When you're painting in the middle of the day it's a good idea to face the sun in order to get more division of light and shade between the vertical and horizontal planes of the scene. This will make a much more interesting picture than if you have your back to the sun and there is a flat light over the whole scene. This kind of flat lighting is all right for a photographer, but usually not for a painter.

The best times of the day for outdoor sketching are early morning and late afternoon. If you're one of those bright-eyed and bushy-tailed characters who love to get up at sunrise and frolic around in the cold gray dawn, the early morning scenes are for you. But I'm afraid that I'm not one of that hearty breed; I really do better work later in the day, perhaps around cocktail time. So you'll see more of my late afternoon and sunset scenes than my early morning pictures. If you're painting in the middle of the day, you can look toward the sun and use the back lighting I've just discussed.

TAKING LIBERTIES WITH COMPOSITION

Sometimes, when you've decided on the scene you want to paint, you find that it makes a perfect composition. In that case, you're lucky and your only problem will be to paint the scene in front of you.

In case the composition is not ideal, you can always eliminate a few objectionable objects or move things around to make a more decorative composition. However, it's a good idea not to make *too many* changes

62

THE POND IN AUTUMN In this autumn scene, the light came from back in the picture, with the water reflecting the light of the sky. The tree in the foreground had reddish brown foliage. Some of the other trees were a dull gold. Collection, Mr. and Mrs. Ernest R. Lavigne.

THE INNER HARBOR In this picture of Rockport's smaller harbor, there is a diffused down light over the entire picture, with the horizontal planes receiving most of the light. Because of the still water, the reflections of boats and wharves are clearly seen.

MARSH'S MILL   This picture was painted in the autumn and is an example of diffused lighting. The gray tone of the sky made a pleasant contrast with the brilliant reds and yellows of the foliage.

in a scene, as you may destroy some of the character of the particular spot that you're painting. If you rearrange too many things in a picture to achieve an ideal composition you'll find that all of your pictures begin to take on a kind of stylized studio arrangement; they all begin to look alike. Outdoor studies generally look a little more unusual than something that you've dreamed up in the studio.

SOME SUGGESTIONS FOR YOUR CONVENIENCE

When painting outdoors, make sure that your canvas is in shadow, because it's impossible to see color correctly if the sun is shining directly on your picture. Sunlight gives a nice warm glow to everything and a sketch that looks warm and brilliant in the sun will look cold and gray when you get it back to the studio. Bright sunlight on canvas is also rather blinding to look at and certainly doesn't do your eyes any lasting good. I generally carry two canvases the same size and put one behind the other on my easel, so that the sun doesn't shine through the canvas on which I'm working. Since I generally work on one canvas in the morning and another one in the afternoon, it's very convenient to have them both on hand when I need them.

After you've selected your subject and are ready to start the picture, be sure that you're in a comfortable spot in which to work. If you stand, try to have a smooth spot to stand on. If you like to paint sitting down, be sure you have a good place for your stool and easel. Someday, some genius will figure out a method of painting lying down. Then we'll really be comfortable.

GEORGETOWN, COLORADO This picture was painted on a rainy day, with the rain clouds partly obscuring the distant mountain. This old mining town was only one of many picturesque spots that we found in Colorado.

6. Outdoor Painting on Location

When you've decided on your composition and you've arranged yourself and your equipment to your satisfaction, then you can start to draw in the picture.

DRAWING THE MAJOR SHAPES

With a brush, a little light blue paint, and lots of medium, draw outlines of the shapes of all the masses of light and dark. This will define the pattern or the framework of the entire picture.

I prefer to do this drawing with a brush and thin paint, instead of using pencil or charcoal. For one thing, you can draw faster with a brush; and you can easily change any of your drawing by rubbing out the lines with your paint rag dipped in a little medium. When you're drawing with charcoal, I think you're just wasting time, because the charcoal dissolves the minute you start to put some paint in over it. If you're going to do an oil painting, you might just as well start working with paint.

BEGINNING TO PAINT

As soon as you've finished drawing in the picture, start right in to paint the sky, rather thinly but in the correct value and color. The sky sets the color and key for the whole painting. Sky color will reflect down into the horizontal planes of the entire picture.

Next, lay in the dark masses, starting at the center of interest. Try to get the right color and value as you go along.

Then put in the medium tones, comparing them to the lightest areas and the darkest darks.

Try to work as directly and as rapidly as you can, paying attention to the relation of one area to another and not bothering with much detail. You can paint thinly, without much finish, but try to cover the whole canvas with approximately the right color and value.

When I am laying in a new picture, I can hardly wait to get the entire canvas covered. I'm sure we all feel the same way about looking at large blank expanses of canvas. Until you get some tone and color over the entire area, you can't tell how the composition will look.

CENTER OF INTEREST

Be careful to keep in mind where the center of interest will be in the picture. It could be a tree, a mountain, or a building; in other words, it's the dominant object that attracted your interest to the scene in the first place.

No other parts of the picture should compete with the center of interest. Everything in the picture should merely lead your eye toward the focal point, where you have your strongest contrasts of tone and color. Always remember: there can be only one center of interest in a picture.

THICK PAINT VERSUS THIN PAINT

It's a good plan to paint rather thinly at first, since you don't want to pile up surplus paint that might get in the way later on. When you've determined the proper shade and color of the different areas, you can paint as heavily as you wish.

Whether you paint heavily or thinly is simply a matter of personal taste. Of course, you want to put enough paint on your canvas so that it won't be too thin and transparent looking. But you don't have to put on big lumps of paint unless you like it that way.

I generally paint my shadows rather thinly, but add heavier paint to the light spots. Many artists pile on the paint with great abandon, sometimes using a palette knife to get a heavy impasto (a thick layer of paint). Their paintings look strong and dramatic. Others use hardly more than a thin stain of paint.

I believe that you can strike a happy medium between these two methods. Certainly whether a canvas succeeds or fails isn't dependent upon the amount of paint you put on it. So, when it comes to your own painting, just do what comes naturally and you'll probably be all right.

FIRST SITTINGS AND SECOND THOUGHTS

Generally I plan to lay in most of the picture at one sitting so that there are only details to finish up later. This is a good idea, since you can't work on the picture all day, due to the change in the light direction.

STEP ONE With a brush, a little blue paint and lots of medium, I draw, in outline, the shapes of all the different objects in the picture: the pond, distant hills, shapes of the branches of the trees, stones in the wall, etc.

STEP TWO I lay in the sky in the right color and value to set the key for the whole picture. In this case, there was so little sky that I decided to include the distant hills also.

STEP THREE   I next put in my important dark spots, starting with the center of interest; namely, the foreground trees and the dark pond beyond them. I also put in the other strong darks; the evergreens, dark fence posts, and dark rocks in the stone wall.

STEP FOUR   Now I add the more subtle tones of the snow shadows and a little more detail in the trees and bushes.

I start one picture in the morning and another one in the afternoon. Some years ago, when I was a little more energetic than I am now, I would even try a third picture after supper. There's one advantage in laying a painting aside before it has been entirely completed: you can better evaluate your work and you can also decide just how much more work is needed to finish it. Sometimes you'll be surprised to find how little more work a picture needs to complete the canvas after your first rough lay-in. I always prefer a picture that is a little unfinished to one in which everything has been completely whittled out. The whole trend of painting today is to get away from the old-time, carefully finished, tight photographic type of picture. A broader, looser, freer, more imaginative style of painting has more charm and is a lot pleasanter to live with than the precisely realistic style.

COMPLETING THE PAINTING

After your first lay-in, you can work all over the picture, but don't change your mind about the color or design of your original composition. Try to think of the picture as a whole and don't overwork any particular areas. When completing the picture, you must be very careful to avoid any details or tones—in either the dark or the light areas—which are so strong that they break up your original light or dark pattern. This pattern must be preserved at all cost.

Try not to clutter up your picture with a lot of unimportant details. It's much better to suggest them than to put them all in. The great advantage an artist has over a photographer is that the artist can leave out anything he wants; he can just concentrate on the important portions of the picture. One advantage of working in big, simple masses with a minimum of detail is that you can work much faster and have a better chance of completing your painting before you lose your original enthusiasm.

COLOR IN OUTDOOR SKETCHING

I would like to mention a few points about color in outdoor sketching.

Your strongest color is usually in your center of interest and in your foreground.

If you're doing a sunlight scene, you'll find a lot of warm color reflected from your sunlight areas into the adjacent shadows. In fact, you

STEP FIVE The completed picture was left in a slightly unfinished state to preserve the sketchy quality that I felt the scene needed. The back lighting in this picture gave me an opportunity to use a warm sky, which made a pleasant contrast with the cool tones of the snow.

can often use warmer color in these shadowy spots than in the sunlit areas.

In painting sunlight, you have to be careful not to get it too warm. It's only the late afternoon sun that has a pinky, orange glow to it. If you paint midday sun with too much warmth in it, you'll find that it has an eggy look.

Generally keep as much warmth as possible in your shadows. This will give them richness and depth. In the shadows, any horizontal surfaces that are open to the sky will pick up some of the cool color of the sky. For instance, flat shadows on snow are often quite cool where the sky can reflect down into them. But under a log or under the eaves of a house, where the sky can't penetrate, the shadow will be quite warm.

When working outdoors in the full light of day, you can intensify slightly the color in your picture, since it will look a little cooler and grayer in the half-light indoors. I hope that the step-by-step painting demonstration in this chapter will help to make all these ideas a little easier to understand.

7. Painting Skies

The sky is the first thing that you paint when you start a picture. The sky sets the key for the entire painting. Sky color reflects down into all the horizontal planes, and the color of the sky helps to determine the character of the whole picture.

SKY COLOR AND ATMOSPHERE

Think of the sky as the interior of a great dome. There is a layer of vapor over the surface of the earth; this vapor grays the sky near the horizon. When you look straight up into the sky, instead of looking at an angle, you see the peak of the dome through the clearest air; that is, you are looking through the thinnest portion of the vapor layer, so you see more of the true color of the sky.

This is why a cloudless sky isn't just blue all over. Its color is affected by layers of vapor and also by the sun. Directly overhead, the sky is a deeper, more intense blue, which changes to a paler blue-green lower in the sky, until finally, near the horizon, the sky becomes a pinky lavender. This gradation makes the sky appear darker overhead and lighter near the horizon. It is also this gradation of color and tone which gives the sky a domed effect.

SKY COLOR AND SUNLIGHT

The blue tones of the sky are further modified by the warm light of the sun, so that you'll find pale pink and pale orange mixed with the blue of the sky.

When you're looking toward the sun—as you frequently do when painting a picture with back lighting—you'll find that the sky is extremely warm and glowing in color. When painting a picture with side lighting, you can generally warm up the sky color as it gets nearer the side from which the light is coming.

CONNECTICUT FARM   In this winter farm scene, the late afternoon sunlight accented the interesting pattern of the cumulus clouds in the sky. I painted most of the sky with the vertical brush strokes that I often use when painting skies.

THE BOUQUET RIVER In this picture of a scene near Elizabethtown, New York, I painted the whole background hill in shadow in order to focus the interest on the river in the foreground and the buildings at the river's edge. Cloud shadows are God's gift to the artist, as they enable him to put nice dark spots in his picture wherever he needs them to improve his composition.

Sometimes the sky opposite the sun will also receive warmth. This is very noticeable at sunset, when you'll see a strong, warm glow on the sky, directly opposite the direction in which the sun is setting.

CLOUDY SKIES

A cloudy sky offers an artist a much better opportunity to compose a fine, decorative arrangement of light and shade. A cloudy sky makes it possible to use cloud shadows throughout the picture, and therefore you can concentrate your light and shade exactly where you want them.

When you're painting clouds, you have to think of their design, color, and value, and how these can tie into the basic pattern of the whole composition.

A sky can add so much to a picture that I believe in showing a generous amount of it. I rarely paint pictures with extremely high horizons. Plenty of sky seems to me to give breadth and atmosphere to the picture.

TYPES OF CLOUDS

In order to paint clouds convincingly, it's necessary to know something about them. While it isn't necessary to remember all their Latin names, it's still advisable to know what various clouds look like and to be able to paint them in their proper color and value.

Clouds form and float at approximately three levels: high, middle, and low.

There are three types of low-lying clouds. *Stratus* means flat, layer-like clouds, generally quite low, and extending horizontally over a relatively large area. *Cumulus* clouds are the puffy, woolly type, having a flat base, and piled up like mountains. *Nimbus* means rain clouds, uniformly gray, and extending over the entire sky.

There can be combinations of these different types of clouds, like Cumulo-Nimbus, or thunderheads; Nimbo-Stratus; or Strato-Cumulus, which cover most of the sky in a simple dark mass.

The middle level clouds are called *Alto*. These can be Alto-Cumulus, which sometimes form a mackerel sky. Alto-Stratus are layer-like clouds, also at the middle level.

The higher clouds are called *Cirrus* and are inclined to be thin, wispy, or feathery, formed of ice crystals. The Cirro-Stratus are fairly uniform layers or sheets. Cirro-Cumulus lie in ripples or ridges across the sky.

AFTERGLOW   This view of Gloucester Harbor was painted from the porch of our cottage at Rocky Neck one summer. Since the light changed so rapidly, I could only paint this subject for a short time each day, and it took me several days to finish the picture. These clouds are a mixture of stratus and cumulus, with a few wind-blown scud clouds near the horizon.

THE ROAD TO HARWINTON   When a sky in the scene you are painting interests you, it is a good idea to feature it and really paint a sky picture. In this painting, the cloud pattern was so interesting that I used a low horizon to feature the sky. The small twigs and branches at the top of the trees give the effect of a gray fuzz and are usually painted to appear that way.

Clouds high in the sky are more brilliant and have more sweeping curves than those lower down in the picture. Clouds nearer the horizon are grayer, lie closer together horizontally, and are decidedly smaller, of course. Just above the horizon, the clouds generally fade into the layer of vapor that is over the earth; they are no longer visible as individual clouds. However, when the air is unusually clear—as it is in the Far West or in the tropics—you can occasionally see individual clouds right at the horizon, with no haze at all.

If you've been able to wade through my more or less scholarly description of the different types of clouds—and if you're still with me—I'd suggest that you just forget all about the correct names, as I do. Just try to remember the appearance of the more common types of clouds that you see in the sky.

PAINTING CLOUDS

Before starting to paint a sky, I carefully study the design of the clouds. I try to pick a pattern that will go with the rest of the picture: a pattern that will carry the lines of interest in the lower part of the picture right up through the sky.

Although clouds give the appearance of standing still, they are actually always in motion. So if you see an effect that you like, get busy and draw it in as rapidly as possible, before it changes. When you have found a cloud pattern you like, stick to it and don't keep trying to find something better; you may not find it, and you'll only waste valuable time that could be spent working on the rest of the picture.

Try to see the clouds that you're painting in simple masses of light and shade. There is considerable warmth in both the light and the shadow areas of the overhead clouds. Those farther away and nearer the horizon should be grayer and cooler, since we know that distance grays and cools all colors.

While painting the sky, don't forget to watch its effect on the rest of the view. You can see where the clouds cast shadows over parts of the scene; you can then make up your mind about what parts of the picture should be light and what parts in shadow. You can use cloud shadows wherever they are needed to give a more colorful or decorative look to the picture.

When painting clouds, use a large brush and paint as freely and loosely as possible, with many soft edges. I paint quite a lot of the sky with vertical brush strokes instead of horizontal ones. In this way, you paint the horizontal clouds with vertical strokes and achieve a looser, more artistic effect that helps to suggest the dome-like look of the sky.

Clouds and their shadows should be painted simply, with hardly any detail. When painting highlights in the light areas, keep them toward the center, well inside the light areas of the clouds.

SOFT AND HARD EDGES

You can suggest modeling in the different cloud masses by the degree of sharpness or softness that you give to the edges. Clouds have much softer edges than you'd think possible. You can paint a whole sky with only one or two sharp touches, letting all the rest of the edges simply melt into each other.

If you're undecided whether an edge is sharp or soft, just squint at it for a moment with your eyes half closed. The soft edges will generally melt together when studied in this manner. As a rule, the greater the contrast between two adjoining masses, the sharper the edges; the less contrast, the softer the edges. If you think that the edge of a cloud is quite sharp, compare it to the silhouette of a tree or mountain against the sky; you'll see that the cloud edge is really fairly soft.

When trying to decide how light or dark to paint the sky, compare it with the strongest lights or the darkest darks in your picture. Skies are often the lightest part of the picture, unless you're painting storm clouds or night scenes. The simplest skies to paint are either light skies with dark clouds, or fairly dark skies with light clouds.

SUNRISES AND SUNSETS

I can never understand why most artists consider the most spectacular kinds of skies—sunrises and sunsets—too mushily sentimental for anyone to try to paint. Maybe we see too many gaudy, calendar-like pictures of sunsets, done by a lot of buckeye artists who try to paint something that will please the general public.

There is nothing wrong with the public's taste in art. Most people, no matter how little they know about art, can usually tell a good picture when they see one. I still think that a sunset, done decoratively and with good taste, makes a marvelous picture. I hope that we'll see more sunrises and sunsets around in the future.

I have picked six different types of clouds more or less at random. The following are illustrations of some of the more familiar types of clouds that I like to paint.

CUMULUS These clouds are a puffy woolly type, having a flat base and piled up like mountains.

STRATUS AND ALTO-STRATUS This is a combination of stratus and alto-stratus clouds, stretching across the sky in flat layers.

STRATUS-CUMULUS These clouds show their top edges slightly shredded by the winds above.

CIRRUS Composed of ice-crystals, cirrus clouds are found high up in the sky.

86

FAIR WEATHER CUMULUS CLOUDS   These clouds produce a wonderfully dramatic
effect to an outdoor setting.

CUMULO-NIMBUS   The lead edge of cumulo-nimbus rain clouds.

8. Trees, Mountains, Water, and Other Landscape Elements

In outdoor painting, trees are probably painted more often than any other objects. Each and every tree has its own and individual characteristics and should be carefully studied. To paint trees well, you should know them well.

STUDYING AND DRAWING TREES

You don't have to be a botanist to paint trees or other shrubbery in a picture. Still, it doesn't hurt to have a good, clear idea of the different characteristics of the more common species of trees that you're liable to see in your local landscape.

It's easier to study the framework or skeleton of a tree in the winter, when the leaves are gone, than in the summer, when the trees are all cluttered up with leaves. In the wintertime, you can see how the branches grow out of the trunk of the tree: whether they grow in an upward sweep or branch out more horizontally, with sharp angles or curves.

When drawing a tree, try to get the character of the *silhouette* of the entire tree. Note whether it's tall and slender or more rounded in form; whether the tree has leaves and twigs. Trees with thin foliage offer an interesting contrast to those with heavy foliage when both are used in the same picture.

PAINTING TREES

When you paint a tree, try to get the character of the particular tree you're painting. Then be sure that it's in scale with the rest of the picture. A tree or a group of trees that forms the center of interest should be mostly inside the edges of the canvas. However, it's all right occasionally to let parts of objects or masses run out of the picture. In their efforts to keep everything inside the confines of the canvas, beginners will often spoil the scale of a tall tree by stunting its height. One way to make a tree look tall is to keep the other elements in the picture—such as stone walls or buildings—down to a scale small enough to make the tree itself look big and impressive.

When you begin to paint trees, get the right pattern of the limbs and branches in their relation to the tree trunks; then get the proper shape of the masses of foliage, which should be painted in a simple pattern of light and shade. Note the direction of light and note where the shadows occur, both in the foliage and on the ground. Next, study the shapes of the shadows, keeping them flat and simple when you paint them in.

Also note the color and value of the light areas of foliage, compared to the parts of the tree in shadow. As a rule, the whole tree, even the light areas, will be darker than the sky. Only when a tree is seen against a dark background—like a hill in shadow or a dark stormy sky—does a tree ever look very light in value.

Don't attempt to put too much detail in the foliage, or draw in all the branches on the tree. Just get the characteristic shape of the whole mass of foliage and don't try to put in every leaf. If you study the outside contour of a mass of leaves and get their right shade and value, you won't have to put much detail in the leaves themselves.

A tree trunk generally looks wider at the ground because of its spreading roots. So be sure that your trees swell out nicely at the ground level and don't look like a lot of posts or telegraph poles.

Another thing to remember is that the branches of a tree grow towards you and away from you, as well as on the sides of the trunk. This means that the branches on the side of the tree facing you must be foreshortened. They should have stronger accents of color or tone to give the effect that they are coming toward you.

I remember one student of mine who always painted trees with all the leaves on the sides, but all the branches and the trunk exposed in the center. It really looked like a fish that had been split in half. The effect was fascinating, but it didn't make a very convincing painting of a tree.

When you're painting distant trees, just think of them as flat spots of color and value, with very little detail. In the wintertime, you see only the trunk and the largest branches, while the smaller branches at the top look like a gray fuzz around the upper part of the tree.

NEPAUG   This autumn scene is an example of trees with heavy foliage contrasted with trees having thin foliage and one tree with bare branches. In this picture all tree-tops are inside the picture. This makes a nice arrangement, but it isn't absolutely necessary to include the entire tree in your picture. You can occasionally run the tree-tops out of the picture, to form the trees in the proper scale with the other elements in the scene.

MT. MANSFIELD It is easier to study the skeleton of a tree in winter than when the tree is all cluttered up with leaves. You can see how the branches grow out of the trunk of the tree, whether they grow with an upward sweep or branch out more horizontally.

THE BIG MAPLE In this autumn scene, the comparatively small size of the house helps to establish the correct size of the trees. Unfortunately, all the brilliant yellows and reds of an autumn scene are completely lost in a black-and-white reproduction.

THE BACK ROAD   As a rule, the foliage of a tree, even in the light areas, will be darker in tone than the sky. It is only when a tree is seen against a dark background that it will look light in value. The dirt road in this picture makes a light note against the darker grass and bushes.

When painting bushes and other shrubbery, just get the correct silhouette of the whole mass of foliage. Then paint it in very simply with a few of the more important branches and twigs to give it the proper shape. Bushes are a little like small trees.

PAINTING ROCKS

I'm always pleased when I get a chance to paint a picture that has rocks or boulders in it. For one thing, rocks have clear-cut shapes and are fun to paint. Their sharp, angular planes also make an interesting contrast with the grass and leaves, which are sometimes soft and mushy looking, especially in the foreground.

When you paint rocks, try to get them the right shape and color. Paint them in simple planes of light and shade in approximately two values. Most rocks are warm gray, though they sometimes vary in different localities.

You can use considerable warmth in all the shadows in rocks, except for rocks that are exposed to cool down-light from the sky. These horizontal planes would be quite cool, of course. When you're about to paint rocks in a stone wall, it helps to decide the general value of the wall in relation to the surrounding areas. Is it mostly a light, medium, or dark spot?

If you paint rocks in a simple, two-toned pattern of light and shade, you'll be surprised how little detail you'll need to make them look completely finished. Just a few halftones in the light and dark areas, and one or two accents, will probably do the trick.

High elevations, such as hills and mountains, have an attraction all their own. Mountains often give an effect of nobility and grandeur that is very impressive.

MOUNTAINS AND HILLS

If a mountain is the main attraction in your picture, it's a good idea to feature this dominant shape by using a low horizon line. Keep trees and other objects in the foreground small and subordinated to the main center of interest.

When you're painting hills or mountains, you want to emphasize their solidity and permanence as well as their height.

You must also remember, when painting hills and mountains, that the lower portions of the mountain extend not only to the right and left

THE TROUT STREAM   When you are painting rocks, try to see them as a simple two-toned pattern of light and dark. When you paint them in this manner, you will be surprised how little detail you need to make them look completely finished.

96

TWIN LAKES, COLORADO (SKETCH) This is a scene that I started to paint, but never finished. I used a fairly low horizon line to make the mountains look more impressive, and added the small foreground figures for the same reason.

of the peaks, but also extend toward you. Picturing this foreshortening is not an easy matter; but it has to be done in order to keep the mountain from looking like a flat, upright plane.

To create the proper recession in this portion of the picture, you sometimes have to use considerable ingenuity in foreshortening forms and arranging color and values. Strong foreground values, contrasted with haze in the distance, help to create the effect of recession in your hills and mountains. Cloud shadows, or shadows cast along canyons or ridges, also help to suggest distance in the picture.

SAND, DIRT, AND DIRT ROADS

Since a lot of weeds, grass, and bushes in the foreground of a scene are rather monotonous, it helps a lot when you are able to find some areas

REFLECTION In this drawing of a man standing at the water's edge, you will notice that his reflection is directly below him in the water. This reflection is as far *below* the water-line as he is *above* it.

of sand or earth for contrast. Dirt is usually a little lighter in appearance than the adjoining grass; the dirt gets a pretty strong down-light from the sky and isn't broken up by a lot of tiny shadows. A dirt road often makes a nice, light pattern, compared with the darker note of the grass and bushes.

PAINTING WATER AND REFLECTIONS

I enjoy painting water in a landscape, perhaps because I have spent a lot of time painting harbor scenes and surf. Or maybe it's because I think that water is just fun to paint.

When you're painting water, think of it as a large mirror lying flat on the ground. Everything above is reflected in the water below. Because water presents a level surface to the sky, the water will take on

VALUES IN WATER This drawing shows the gradation in the values of the water. As you look down into the water in the foreground, you see the greenish color of the water itself or the color of the sandy or muddy bottom. Further back in the picture, the water reflects more of the color of the sky and is consequently lighter in value, with an occasional brilliant reflection forming on a ripple. In the distance, the water may look faintly darker, with alternating strips of light and dark tones.

GALLOWS BAY   This is a picture of a schooner at Christiansted in the Virgin Islands. Since the boat was moving, I didn't have time to get more than a general impression of the scene. There are probably a few reflections that I didn't completely finish.

AT THE WEST BRANCH   This autumn scene of the Farmington River loses a lot in a black-and-white reproduction. The yellows, oranges, and reds are all reflected in the still river.

the color of the sky, except when you're close at hand; then, when you look down into the water, you see the greenish color of the water itself, or the sandy or muddy bottom.

If you keep a few simple points in mind, I'm sure you won't have any trouble painting water. Remember that the reflection of any object is directly below it in the water, as far below the water line as the object is above the line.

Water is not a perfect reflecting surface; it's rather like an old mirror that has turned green with age. As a result, reflections of light objects will look a little darker; reflections of medium-toned objects will look about the same value; while the reflection of a dark object will look a little lighter than the object itself.

In painting a fairly large body of water, such as a lake or river, you'll notice that the nearby water appears darker when you look down into it; this is because there is less reflected light from the sky to brighten it. A little farther away, the water is lighter, with an occasional brilliant reflection on a ripple.

Still farther away, the water may look slightly darker, with alternating horizontal strips of light and dark tones. These various tones are caused by areas of smooth water in contrast to the rougher areas that are ruffled by the wind. Or in a stream, they are caused by the current of the water. The smooth areas reflect either the sky or objects directly above the water, while the rougher portions reflect light from many directions. You can paint these areas like long, horizontal wedges of alternating lighter and darker tone; be careful to keep them narrower and closer together as they recede in the distance.

There are a lot of other objects that you will want to paint in landscapes, but we'll talk about them in a later chapter.

9. Farms, Towns, and Cities

After painting landscapes for many years, I've discovered that pictures with buildings or figures in them are generally more popular with the public than landscapes which consist merely of scenery. I think the reason is that people are interested in everything concerning other people, such as their houses, barns, or anything else related to other human beings. I've often observed that when someone walks into an art exhibition, the first pictures he looks at are usually portraits or figure compositions. Even though a figure in a picture may not be the center of interest, your eye is always attracted to it.

BUILDINGS

I know you can paint an interesting landscape without including any signs of human habitation. There's nothing wrong with nature just as it is, without any man-made improvements. But you'll probably include buildings in your pictures often, so I'll touch briefly on a few points that may be helpful in drawing them.

To make buildings look convincing, be sure to draw them in the right perspective. As you'll remember, the receding lines of all objects above the horizon line will go down to a vanishing point on the horizon, while everything below the horizon line will go up to meet it. Wherever your eye line is in the picture, that is the horizon line, of course. The drawing of the houses on the hillside on page 104 will make this clear.

When drawing buildings, try to get their proper silhouette. At the same time, study the light and shadow on each building; be careful to paint the shadows the right color and value in relation to the light areas of the buildings. Then be sure the buildings are in scale with the trees and other objects in the picture.

FARM SCENES

A great many farm buildings are painted red. This gives you a chance to make use of some fine, warm color in your picture. As there is usually quite a lot of green in most farm scenes, the red note makes a pleasant contrast to the color of the rest of the painting. Though artists have been painting so many red barns over the years that it has almost become a joke, barns are just as paintable as ever; I don't think the public will ever tire of them. However, buildings that are exposed to the weather for some time generally have a slightly faded appearance. So don't use too brilliant a red when painting farm buildings; your picture will be much more artistic if you gray the color somewhat. Occasionally, when there is a strong down-light, the roofs of the buildings will be a lighter note than the rest of the buildings. This is especially noticeable if you're painting a rainy day scene.

It's a good idea to put in some of the debris and junk that you often see around a farm: old farm equipment, broken-down hay wagons, harrows, tractors, and so forth. In New England, it used to be a familiar sight to see the porch of every farmhouse decorated by an old icebox with no door on it, or a sofa with the springs all falling out. This isn't the case with prosperous farms, where everything is neat and tidy and not a bit picturesque. I think that all artists enjoy painting buildings that are old and ramshackle-looking. The shiny new ones haven't the charm of the decrepit old wrecks.

Near our studio, here in New Hartford, Connecticut, there is a farm that was practically falling apart. It hadn't been painted or repaired in years. We all used to love to paint it until it was sold to some city people, who just ruined it by fixing it up.

I sometimes take a few liberties with farm buildings that I'm painting and make them look a little more weather-beaten than they really are. This may not make any hit with the owner of the place, who hates to see his shiny buildings grow old so rapidly, but it makes the scene more fun to paint.

Horizon  Vanishing Point

VERMONT VILLAGE   In this picture of the Vermont village there is a high horizon line, and the receding lines of all objects vanish at different points on the horizon line. I hope I have made clear that in a picture with hills or mountains, the horizon line wouldn't be along the top edge of the hills, but would be a lower line at the level of the viewer's eye line. In this picture, I think the horizon line would be at the level of the top line of the church's roof. Collection, Dr. and Mrs. A. Rocke Robertson.

CHIP BUCKIN'S PLACE   When I was painting this nice old Florida cabin, I found I was being eaten alive by some invisible insects that left bites all over me resembling large freckles. When I asked Chip why the bugs didn't bite him instead of concentrating on me, he said they only bit "damn Yankees." I didn't believe him, because I think the bugs had tried to bite him, but were unable to make a dent in his tough hide which looked exactly like tanned leather.

I found the Spanish moss quite interesting to paint. Its color changes during the day, depending on whether the moss is wet or dry. Collection, Dr. John Houlihan.

106

MOUNTAIN FARM   This farm near Elizabethtown, New York, was painted just as the sky started to clear at the end of a rainy day. The picture is in tones of blues and greens. The farm-house was a kind of dirty yellow and the barns a grayish brown.

Village street scenes are always interesting to paint. In Rockport, Massachusetts, where we spend our summers, you can always see a number of artists busily engaged in painting the winding streets, the big trees, and the picturesque old houses. Churches also look handsome in the village scene, with their graceful steeples and their air of peace and dignity.

When you're about to paint a village street scene, decide on the pattern of light and shade. If you're sketching in the summertime, the dark tree trunks, foliage, dark roofs of houses, grass, and shadow might be part of your dark pattern. The sky, with the sunlight on the houses, road, and grass, could be part of your light pattern.

When painting shadows on a house or road, keep them just as flat as possible, with hardly any modeling or detail in them. In other words, just let them be a simple pattern of dark in the right color and value. When painting shadows on roads, keep the edges rather sharp, particularly the edge of the shadow nearest you. This will bring the edge towards you and give the effect of the shadow lying *flat* on the road. Try to have your strongest contrasts of color near the part of the picture that is your center of interest.

CITY SCENES

When it comes to painting city scenes, there are any number of fascinating subjects to choose from.

Because of the somewhat standardized architecture of many city buildings, I think that you can get a more interesting picture by painting the scene with some dramatic lighting or atmospheric effect. A street scene with most of the picture in shadow, and some light just hitting the center of interest—which could be a building or a group of figures—is often very effective.

The same view on a rainy or foggy day might be well worth painting. Most artists like to paint a rainy day picture in which the wet sidewalks and streets reflect objects like a mirror. Details are more or less lost; thus, you can easily work out an interesting black-and-white tonal arrangement of figures, cars, lamp posts, and buildings, with a little toplight reflecting down from the sky.

THE CITY   This is one of many New York harbor scenes I painted for the Kennedy Galleries. I tried to get the character and atmosphere of the scene without painting it in a photographic manner. New York is a marvelous town but, to coin a phrase, most of us would rather visit the place than have to live there. Courtesy, The Kennedy Galleries.

If it's a night scene that interests you, all kinds of possibilities can be worked out with street lights, signs, and the dark notes of buildings and figures.

Of course, all these atmospheric effects have to be painted from memory later in your studio. I'll have more about this in the chapter on studio painting.

FIGURES IN LANDSCAPES

A picture can often be improved by the addition of a figure or two. Not only do figures help establish the scale of other objects in the picture, but they lend interest to the rest of the scene.

It's often a good idea to spot figures near the center of interest, or at least have them looking in that direction. You'll find that the glance of the viewer usually follows the direction in which the figures in the picture are facing. If you have trouble deciding just where you want to place a figure, it sometimes helps if you make a small cardboard cut-out of the figure, and move it around on the canvas until the placement looks right.

A figure in a picture should be started as a dark silhouette. Be sure that you get the right action in the figure, as if it were engaged in some familiar activity, such as walking or carrying something. The minute you see the figure, you should understand just what it's doing. Don't attempt to model the figure; let it be just a flat pattern.

If you want to give the effect of more detail, you can paint part of the figure in a lighter or darker tone. For instance, if you wanted to paint the figure of a farmer carrying a pail of milk, you might paint him with a flat, dark coat and light tan trousers. His head and hands would be just reddish-brown spots, his cap a yellow note. It's surprising how little detail is required when painting figures in this manner.

However, you must be careful that the figure or figures are not painted too strongly. Be sure that they are carefully integrated into the design of the rest of the picture. If you look at a figure out in a field or on a street, it's almost always a medium-dark note, compared to the surrounding areas. It's only occasionally that you'll need to put a little top lighting on a figure. However, when your picture needs an accent of bright color, you might use a figure wearing a shirt or jacket in red— or some other brilliant color—to add interest to the scene.

THE VILLAGE CHURCH   In a village street scene, a church makes a pleasing center of interest. I used the small figures to add interest to the scene. I tried to paint most of the figures as simple dark silhouettes. This started out to be a picture of Cleaves Street in Rockport, Massachusetts, but I took a few liberties with the scene, moving trees around and changing a few houses to improve the composition. I hope the result has justified my efforts.

When you're painting a group of people, always paint them as a large irregular dark mass. Be careful to have the outside silhouette of the group look convincing. Here again, if you wish to give the effect of more detail in the figures, you can vary the values or color of some of their clothing. When you look at a group of people, you get only the general impression of the whole crowd; your imagination has to supply all the missing details.

RAINY DAY   In this scene of New York in the rain, I tried merely to suggest the figures and other objects in the picture. I think a picture that requires a little study is more interesting than one in which the meaning is obvious at first glance.

CITY LIGHTS   In this night scene of New York City, I tried to suggest a little of the movement and glamour of the theatrical district after dark. The figures are only an irregular dark mass, with the silhouette of the group suggesting individual figures. I can't find a single letter in the electric signs. Can you?

10. Painting the Seasons

The great French impressionist, Monet, used to paint the same scene over and over again, using many different light effects and color schemes. He painted haystacks and his lily pool many times. I've often thought what fun it would be to take some favorite scene and paint it in different seasons of the year. So far, I've never had time to do it, but maybe some day I'll get around to trying it.

THE IMPORTANCE OF PAINTING FROM NATURE

In many parts of the country, it's quite uncomfortable to work outdoors in the winter; a lot of one's painting has to be done in the studio. As a result, most of us can hardly wait for spring and a chance to get outdoors again.

While work in the studio is important, nature is the real source of inspiration. It's absolutely necessary for an artist to do just as much outdoor painting as possible. There is nothing that can take the place of first-hand study of a scene outdoors. When you make a sketch of a scene—even a pencil sketch—you'll learn a lot more about your subject than if you merely took a photograph of the same view. So, as soon as the weather permits, pack up your painting equipment and get right to work outside.

Let's talk about some of the interesting effects that you see when you paint landscapes in the different seasons of the year.

SPRING LANDSCAPES

A spring landscape, with its lovely delicate colors and soft atmospheric tones, is a fascinating subject to paint. Later in the summer the greens get a bit monotonous; but in the spring, the color is fresh and varied.

The soft, hazy spring atmosphere gives everything a delicate charm and produces some lovely, pearly grays, especially in the more distant parts of the picture. This enveloping atmosphere makes it easy for you to get a pleasing harmony of color, because there is a little of this warm

SPRING ON COTTON HILL   In this spring landscape, you can see the pale green of the new leaves, while some of the trees still in bud have a pinkish look, almost like autumn coloring. There are still some reddish browns in the foreground grass, bushes, and the distant hills. The values of the distant hills are a good example of aerial perspective.

THE WINDING RIVER In this panoramic view of the Bouquet River in the Adirondacks, we have a typical green summer scene. I used some warmth in the foreground shadows, in the trees, and in their reflections in the river. As they recede into the distance, I added more of the cool color of the atmosphere until the distant mountains were in shades of gray-blue, thus getting away from the all-pervading green of most summer landscapes.

116

gray mixed with many of the local colors in the picture. In the early spring, when some of the trees are still in bud, they often have a pinkish look, almost like autumn coloring. This warm color goes very well with the pale greens, yellows, and soft grays of the rest of the picture.

Spring coloring is delicate, and quite a bit of study is required to match the color and values of the scene in front of you. As usual, your strongest colors and values should be in the foreground or at the center of interest. But there probably won't be very brilliant color in the picture or a very strong contrast of light and dark. The whole picture will be in the lighter part of your value scale, with your darks considerably grayed up. Due to the soft enveloping atmosphere, there will be no strong pattern of sunlight and shadows.

Unless it's handled in a rather broad and simple manner, a spring scene can look too pretty for words. However, I don't think that the fault lies in the subject matter; it's merely the fault of the artists who have painted spring scenes in such a trite and sentimental manner.

When you go sketching in the spring, try to see if you can capture on your canvas just a little of the charm of this loveliest time of the year.

SUMMER LANDSCAPES

My only objection to painting a summer landscape is that it's sometimes difficult to avoid getting the whole picture too green. In very thickly wooded areas, about all you can see is green grass and green leaves on the trees and bushes. Try to find some scene that has a little distance in it; then you can paint the distant greens with more atmospheric color in them. This atmosphere will turn them into blue-greens, blues, and lavenders.

You can also use a little cool sky color on the horizontal planes of various objects in the picture, as well as on the tops of trees and bushes. By warming up the shadows that are not exposed to the sky, particularly those in the foreground, you can introduce a little more warmth, which will give variety to the color in the rest of the picture. You can also use warm touches in the earth and in lots of weeds and shrubs.

ATMOSPHERIC EFFECTS IN SUMMER

Of course, if you're painting any particular time of day or a particular atmospheric effect, then you have nothing to fear from the prevailing green. For instance, if you're painting a late afternoon scene, the warm orange sunlight will cast a glow over the whole picture; this warm glow serves to neutralize many of the greens. Some of the shadows might be quite cool, so you can get a pleasant effect of warm and cool color in your painting.

If you're painting a foggy or rainy day, the down-light from the sky will reflect down into every part of the scene and will modify the greens and other local colors. You'll end up with more of a harmony in gray.

In a sunset scene, the brilliant sky will be the center of interest; the rest of the landscape will be so toned down that the local color of the trees, grass, and other foliage will not be too assertive.

A scene with back lighting—when you're looking *into* the sun, with light hitting the top of all the objects in the picture—generally has a warm sky. This warmth radiates through the rest of the picture and adds warm color to all the horizontal planes. If you're painting in the middle of the day, you'll find that a back light is the only successful way to paint many scenes. Your upright planes in shadow will count as dark notes against the horizontal planes in light; you'll have a chance to tie your darks together into the simple pattern which is needed to produce a good picture.

When you're trying to paint a sunset or some other rapidly changing atmospheric effect, you'll find that it will be gone before you can capture it on canvas. In this case, if you make a quick sketch of the scene, approximating the important colors and values, you'll be able to finish the picture later in the studio. The notes that you make on the spot will help you later to recall the important characteristics of the scene.

Sometimes you can roughly lay in your pattern of light and dark, plus the important color notes, on your large canvas, then complete it the next day. Otherwise, a pencil sketch and some color notes will often be all you need to produce a convincing picture in the studio.

SUMMER HEADACHES

Occasionally, there are a few difficulties that bother an artist when painting landscapes in the summer. For one thing, just carrying one's painting equipment around is quite a job. Sometimes, by the time you've found the ideal spot to paint you're so bushed that you have hardly enough energy left to start painting. I find that as I get older, it isn't as much fun crawling through barbed-wire fences as it was in my

THE ROAD TO NEPAUG In this autumn scene, the trees were painted in tones of red, orange, and yellow. The grass and bushes were warm greens and yellows. The distant hills were lavender blue. I used a grayish sky which helped offset the brilliance of the rest of the picture. Collection, Mr. and Mrs. Albert H. Baudouin.

younger days. Then, about the time that you've picked out the spot you want to paint and have all your equipment nicely arranged, it's either time to eat lunch or it's starting to rain.

Whenever I can, I park my station wagon as near as possible to my painting location, so that I have a handy spot to retire to in case of emergency.

AUTUMN LANDSCAPES

A fall scene is hard to paint because all the brilliant colors in nature are difficult to capture on canvas. When you look at an autumn landscape, it's a beautiful sight. But when you try to reproduce it, you often find that your finished picture looks cheap and gaudy; the colors are much too bright.

If you want to avoid buck-eye calendar effect, it's necessary to go easy and not use too much brilliant color. If you keep the colors a bit subdued, you'll be able to get a more pleasing effect and a painting in better taste.

Because of its warm colors, an autumn landscape is an almost universal favorite. The reds, greens, oranges, and purples of an autumn scene make a striking spot of color on the wall of anyone's home. There is so much interest in interior decoration these days that people are very color-conscious. They are inclined to pick out a picture that will go with the color scheme of their room or a picture that picks up the color of a couch or a favorite rug.

Of course, the ideal way to decorate a room is to start with a painting you like and then plan all the furnishings to go with the picture. I've occasionally had the good luck to have someone plan a room around one of my pictures. It's very gratifying to have anyone like your work so much; it makes you feel that it's a pleasure and a privilege to be an artist.

CONTROLLING AUTUMN COLOR

One way to avoid too much gaudy color is to paint the scene on a gray day, when the sky will modify the brilliant color and produce a more subtle harmony. Fog or mist also gives a pleasant atmospheric effect to an autumn landscape.

CREEK NEAR THOMASTON   The colors of this autumn scene were warm brown and orange with some greens in parts of the foliage and in the water. The light spots in the right foreground were rocks and orange-pink floating leaves. The sky was a warm gray, while the distant hill was a grayish purple. Collection, Mr. and Mrs. Ernest R. Lavigne.

But if you wish to paint the scene in brilliant sunlight, it's wise to have a good deal of the picture in shadow, with just a portion of the scene in brilliant light.

I've had better luck with my own paintings of fall scenes when the landscape wasn't all a riot of color. When a few of the trees have lost their leaves, the trees with bare branches make a nice contrast with those that are still covered with foliage. A picture that has its brilliant color concentrated in some particular spots is generally more interesting than one with bright color all over the canvas.

WINTER LANDSCAPES

When you think of a winter scene, a snow scene generally comes to mind. The white of the snow makes a dramatic light contrast to all the dark objects in the picture; without half trying, you can work out a fine black-and-white pattern for your picture.

As a rule, a snow scene is either sharp and brilliant, with considerable black-and-white contrast, or it's soft and atmospheric. Either effect can make an interesting picture.

Usually, the lightest part of a snow scene will be the snow itself. The sky should be toned down a little to give full emphasis to the light pattern of the snow. However, if you're doing a sunrise or sunset and you want to portray a brilliant sky, then you have to consider that the snow is more or less in shadow; you have to keep the snow toned down in order to concentrate the viewer's interest on the sky.

LIGHT AND COLOR ON SNOW

Snow, by reason of its whiteness, is a perfect reflector of light from any direction. In the middle of the day, the warm glow of the sun gives the snow a slightly yellowish cast. Later in the day, the snow will be closer to pale orange or pink. On the snow exposed to the sky, the flat shadows are quite blue. The combination of the warm sunlight areas and the cool shadows gives the snow a great deal of brilliance.

When you're painting a picture that has the sunlight coming from either side, or from a low angle behind you, you'll find that the relatively upright planes facing the sun will be the lightest part of the snow. The relatively horizontal planes will have a delicate halftone over them. This halftone can be a pale yellow or blue, or sometimes a faint lavender.

VERMONT SKETCH   I made this sketch of the Vermont village at the same time that I did *Vermont Village* (page 105). I thought the other picture was more interesting with a covered bridge in the lower right foreground. In a snow scene it is easy to work out a simple two-toned pattern of light and dark. Some of the buildings, the trees, and distant hills are the darks, while the snow and some of the houses are the white pattern.

THE WINTER BROOK In this picture of the winding stream, the light is coming from a low angle behind me. As a result, the relatively upright planes of the snow are the lightest part of the picture. The more nearly horizontal planes, receiving less light, have a delicate tone over them.

THE OLD HOMESTEAD This farm scene near Montgomery Village, Vermont, was painted in the spring when the water from the melted snow was starting to flood all the small creeks and rivers.

As long as the main light areas of the snow are toned down just a little bit and the more upright planes stand out as light notes, the snow will look solid and convincing.

In the late afternoon, the areas of snow in sunlight are pale, pinkish orange, which contrasts with the large, cool shadow areas of the rest of the picture.

RANDOM NOTES ON WINTER PAINTING

Masses of bare trees on a hillside are a purplish brown or gray, except when they are in brilliant sunlight; then they take on a pink or orange color. The evergreens are always a warm, dark green, and make an excellent contrast to the white snow.

Willow trees—particularly weeping willows, with their many small branches—are a yellowish tan, which stands out as a lighter note in contrast to the darker browns and grays of the other trees.

In snow, any shadows that are not exposed to the top-light of the sky will often be quite warm. They will be especially warm if there is a nearby object in sunlight—like a house or a tree—that can reflect warmth into the shadow areas of the snow.

If there is no sunlight in the picture, the snow will be a coolish white. It will be a delicate gray if the clouds are dark.

Snow clinging to the branches and boughs of evergreen trees frequently makes fascinating designs against dark backgrounds.

When a thaw has set in, the warm orange, red, and yellow tones of the exposed grass and bushes make a colorful pattern against the remaining patches of snow.

A winter scene without snow has a somber charm of its own. The bare trees are often very decorative when contrasted with the faded tans and browns of the earth, grass, and bushes; this combination produces a distinguished color harmony.

Even the wintry skies have a beauty all their own. A winter scene consisting of browns, grays, and tans is sometimes transformed when the late afternoon sunlight floods the whole picture with warmth; the sun makes a glowing color harmony out of what might otherwise have been a rather drab landscape.

MOUNTAIN LAUREL   In late June the mountain laurel is beautiful. This laurel was painted on a rocky hillside near our Connecticut studio.

11. Atmospheric Effects

As I mentioned in the chapter on painting skies, I like sunsets and think they are fascinating subjects to paint. However, they are difficult, because you are trying to paint light itself; with the limited range of oil paints, you can only approximate the brilliance you see before you.

PAINTING SUNSETS

The fact that a sunset lasts such a short time makes it necessary to do most of the painting from memory, later in the studio. A quick sketch

STEP ONE   I start by drawing in outline the shape of all the objects in the picture. I use a little blue paint and a lot of medium, as usual, and draw with a fairly small brush. This is just as easy as doing a charcoal drawing of the scene. I think that if you are going to paint, you might as well start right in and paint with a brush.

of the pattern of light and dark, with notes of the color of the different areas, will help you remember the scene and record it the next day.

A sunset is simply a landscape with back lighting; you have to look directly into it to see the most brilliant color. The sky will be the center of interest; the rest of the picture must be toned down to a more or less dark pattern to contrast with the light of the sky. The pattern is two-toned; the sky is the light note and the rest of the picture is dark.

In a sunset, it's better not to show the sun itself, but to have it hidden behind some clouds or just below the horizon. In this way, you can paint the other areas of the picture—those that are in the direct rays of the sun—as light as you wish, and you can still imagine that the sun is even lighter.

In my old days as an illustrator, when we wanted to paint some people around a campfire at night, we'd always have the fire itself concealed

STEP TWO I lay in the sky in the correct color and value. I always paint the sky first, because it sets the key for the entire picture. Some of the sky color is reflected down into the horizontal planes of the picture.

by some figure or some object in the foreground; we'd just show the firelight on the figures sitting around the fire. This light could be very bright and would still look very convincing.

When the sun is a little *below* the horizon, there is a brilliant glow of color just *above* the horizon, but your strongest light is on the clouds a little way up in the sky. It's difficult to get enough strength of color in the sky and, at the same time, keep the sky light enough. To do this, you'll have to use considerable white with some of the low-key colors, like orange and red.

A sunset sky will often start with a brilliant orange or red at the horizon, changing to a pale yellow, then to a delicate green, and farther up in the sky, to a dark blue. The warm light from the sky, reflecting down into the picture, gives a pleasant glow to the whole scene.

While a sunset is generally a warm picture, there'll be plenty of cool

STEP THREE   I lay in the broad masses of light and shade, although I don't attempt to get the correct values of all the darks. At this point I try to establish the black-and-white pattern of the composition. This is the first moment when the pattern of the picture is clearly defined.

colors that will complement the warm notes. The portions of the scene that don't receive the warm glow from the setting sun will be cool. As a result, there will be cold blues, greens, and purples in the parts of the clouds that are shielded from the sun's direct rays. There will also be cool shadows in other parts of the picture, caused by the cold blue light of the sky directly overhead.

As the sky is the most important part of a sunset picture, be sure that you have a decorative spotting of your lights and darks in the sky and that the color harmony has been carefully worked out.

PAINTING TWILIGHT

I think that the loveliest time of day is just before dusk, at twilight. There is a mysterious quality that appeals to me. I particularly like the simple pattern of light and shade that you see just before dark. There

STEP FOUR   I further develop the color and tone of the different portions of the dark areas, making sure that they are correct in color and value. I do the same thing with the light areas also. At this point, the picture is almost finished.

is very little detail, except in the foreground or the center of interest, and there are lots of lost edges and soft edges all over the picture.

The whole scene can be painted in just a couple of tones, with a very simple color scheme, probably consisting of two analogous colors. However, be sure that there is a decorative arrangement of the light-and-dark pattern of the picture. A brief pencil sketch of the pattern of light and shade, with notes on the color of the larger areas of the picture, will help you to remember the scene. If you try to paint it the next day, while you still remember it, you'll often be able to paint a very convincing twilight scene.

NIGHT SCENES

Night scenes provide some fascinating subjects for an artist to paint. I think that one of the most beautiful sights in nature is a moonlit landscape. Nothing could be more mysterious or romantic. This probably accounts for the great popularity of moonlit scenes with the public.

When you paint a moonlit landscape, there are a few points that should be remembered. For one thing, moonlight is much cooler and weaker than sunlight. You can see the big masses of light and shade, but their edges are often very soft or entirely lost; there is little detail in either the light or the shadows. The many soft or lost edges give a fascinating effect of unreality and mystery to the scene.

Due to the comparative weakness of the light, there is nothing very light in the picture. This kind of picture would be at the darker end of the value scale.

We've all seen alleged moonlight pictures that were simply daylight scenes painted blue. When we study moonlight and see how it really looks, we find that there is very little blue in a moonlight scene. There is a great deal of warmth, particularly in the shadows. You can use a purplish brown in some of the shadows, while a grayed-up blue or green is plenty cool enough for the sky. As a matter of fact, a little warmth can be mixed with almost everything in the picture. Even strong local colors are so toned down by moonlight that they count more as values than as definite colors.

Be sure to have the moon itself behind some clouds, or else just above the top of the canvas. The moon's location can be indicated by a slightly warm blur of light at the top of the canvas, extending down a little way

THE ESSEX MARSHES   This is the complete picture with the details carried as far as I thought necessary. It is a good idea not to overwork a picture. I think a painting which looks almost unfinished is more attractive than one which is completely whittled out with a high commercial finish.

TWILIGHT   A twilight scene can be almost a two-toned pattern of dark and light. The sky and the light road are the light pattern, while everything else is a part of the dark design. If you squint at the scene through half-closed eyes, all of the darks melt together into one large dark mass. The lights also stand out as a definite light pattern.

MOONLIGHT BAY This is a portion of the harbor below our studio at Pigeon Cove, Massachusetts. You often see a lobsterman working with his gear near the old fishhouse. Rockport, which is across the bay, has not been shown in this picture.

into the picture. I think that it's best to use back lighting in most moon-light scenes.

The only time I like to see the moon in a picture is when the setting sun provides the general light for the entire scene. In this case, the moon is not the source of light; the moon can be used as a decorative spot that has no noticeable effect on the rest of the picture.

Night scenes featuring lights other than the light of the moon can be very interesting. Street scenes that feature a variety of artificial lights have distinct pictorial possibilities. Even fireworks, as Whistler so ably demonstrated in his *Nocturnes,* can make a beautiful and imaginative picture.

FOG SCENES

A fog scene is a lot of fun to paint.

Owing to the density of the atmosphere, all objects become grayer as they move farther away in the picture; they quickly become simple spots of light and shade, and finally vanish completely. This gives you a chance to silhouette your foreground and middle distance against the light-gray background. Because there is nothing in the background to detract from the center of interest, you'll find it very easy to evolve a striking two-toned pattern of light and dark.

You can paint the foreground in full color with strong contrasts. This will emphasize the grayness and softness of the rest of the picture. It will also prevent the picture from looking too pale and fuzzy.

It's quite permissible to assume that a little warm light is breaking through in the foreground or the center of interest; this makes a pleasant color contrast with the more muted color farther back in the picture. At a little distance, objects lose all details and appear as light or dark silhouettes. The gray background isn't a cold gray, but is a little more on the warm side. Once in a while, the fog takes on a pale lavender or delicate pink color. There is a diffused down-light on everything in the picture; this light makes a nice contrast between the horizontal top planes of objects and the darker upright planes of the rest of the picture. When you're painting a scene with down-light, it might help to think of the light as a thin layer of snow on all the top planes in the picture.

RAINY DAYS

A rainy day scene should also be painted with a down-light; but the top horizontal planes of all objects in the picture, being wet, will be lighter

THE MOTIF   I thought we ought to include one picture of the famous old fish-house on the wharf at Rockport, Massachusetts. It has been painted so often and is such a popular subject for artists from all over the country that it is known as Motif No. 1. A fog scene is interesting to paint, as the foreground and middle distance stand out effectively against the light gray background. Distant objects either vanish or are seen only as vague silhouettes through the fog. This adds a pleasing air of mystery to the picture.

and somewhat shiny. The horizontal planes will act like mirrors and will reflect objects directly above them.

The sky will be a darker shade of gray. The lower edges of some of the clouds will be very soft where the rain is falling.

The visibility in the picture is better than in a fog scene, but you'll find that distant portions of the picture will be only simple silhouettes of tone, with very few details.

The roofs of buildings, when wet, will reflect a lot of the sky color. For this reason, roofs should be painted as very light spots, except when you're painting a roof of old wooden shingles. Such a roof absorbs a good deal of water and has a dark, porous texture that doesn't reflect the light from the sky.

Puddles in a road, yard, or street are a great help in painting a rainy day scene. They reflect anything that is directly above them, such as trees, houses, or sky. Remember, if the puddle reflects the sky and is a light spot, it should have a dark edge; a dark puddle is more likely to have an edge of light separating the puddle from the medium light of the road or street.

PAINTING STORMS

A storm scene can be immensely dramatic, but it will have to be done from memory. It isn't any fun to be out in a real storm, let alone trying to paint it. From the comparative comfort of a car, it's possible to make pencil notes of the black-and-white pattern and important color areas.

As you study the scene, emphasize the important features of the storm. The dark dramatic sky, and the trees bending before the wind, all help to portray one of nature's most impressive and awesome sights. The picture will probably be low-keyed, but you can have strong contrasts and a dramatic light on your center of interest, which can be practically spotlighted.

When I'm out watching a storm, my mind is generally divided between studying the dramatic cloud effects and wondering whether lightning really strikes only once in the same spot. After living in the country for some time, I think that lightning does strike in the same spots. I don't want to be in any of those target areas in a thunderstorm. However, storm scenes are interesting to paint. I suggest that you try one and see what you can do with nature's most exciting and spectacular stage effect.

APRIL SHOWERS   There is better visibility in a rainy day picture than in a fog scene, although distant objects are a little bit grayed up by the moisture in the atmosphere. By using plenty of reflections on the horizontal surfaces, you can give the effect of wetness. In this picture the forsythia is in bloom, but the trees are only budding and haven't started to leaf out.

APPROACHING STORM   The ominous dark sky and the wind-swept foliage help to give the effect of an approaching storm. Storms are dramatic and exciting to paint. Sometimes juries at art exhibits prefer them to more placid landscapes.

12. Painting in the Studio

At least nine tenths of all the pictures exhibited throughout the country have been painted in a studio, usually from sketches, photographs or other material obtained outside, on location. I'm referring, of course, to the work of the leading professional artists in the country. However, their ability to paint realistically and convincingly *indoors* is the result of their thorough knowledge of nature, gained through hours of *outdoor* sketching and painting.

Years ago, when I quit illustrating and moved up to the country to live, I painted all my landscapes outdoors and rarely put a brush stroke on them in the studio. I still do a lot of work outside, and I think these pictures have a realism and honesty that a lot of studio work lacks.

ADVANTAGES OF PAINTING INDOORS

When you're painting a picture in the studio, it's easier to concentrate on the important elements of the picture, such as composition, color, and general mood of the scene. You can eliminate all the unessential details. This helps you paint a simpler, more personal interpretation of the scene: an interpretation with more dramatic impact. It's sometimes possible to work out a more pleasing composition, or a simpler color scheme, when you're away from the actual scene. You have a chance to be less literal and more creative.

When you're working outdoors, you're generally so busy trying to record exactly what you see that you haven't time to do much more than make a literal copy of the scene before you. This is perfectly all right, as it's necessary to be thoroughly familiar with the appearance of everything you wish to include in your picture. Of course, the best way to gain this information is to sketch and paint constantly outdoors.

OUTDOOR PAINTING IS THE FOUNDATION

Many of my pictures are painted in the studio these days; but if it hadn't been for the hundreds of outdoor sketches that I've always made, it would be impossible for me to get any truth or consistency into my studio work. You can get into some bad painting habits if you stay away from nature too long. Nature, after all, is your main source of inspiration.

Of course, working conditions are much more comfortable in the studio. You can arrange your painting equipment to better advantage. If you want to paint a fairly large picture, it's much easier to do it indoors. I used to carry large canvases around outside, and try to keep them from blowing away while I worked on them. This was a lot of good, clean fun, but I still think that it's better to paint the big ones inside where the weather is more temperate.

SOME SUGGESTIONS FOR WEEKEND PAINTERS

I realize that the amateur or weekend painter, whose opportunities to paint outdoors are limited, may find it necessary to do a lot of his paint-

STEP ONE This is the first stage of a picture that I painted in the studio from a sketch I made in New Hampshire. I started with the usual outline drawing of the shapes of the main elements in the picture, following the same method that I use in all of my work.

142

ing at home. But I know any spare time that can be spent painting *out-doors*—on weekends, after work, or on holidays—will be most rewarding and will provide invaluable reference material for your *indoor* painting.

Your studio pictures will have to be painted from material that you've obtained outdoors. Sketches, photographs, or occasionally written notes will sometimes help you recall some fleeting impression long enough to capture it on canvas.

SKETCHES VERSUS PHOTOGRAPHS

With my own studio painting, I have better luck working from outdoor sketches than from photographs. If you take the time to draw a scene, you know a lot more about every object in it than if you merely snap a photo.

I know that my own photographs are invariably disappointing when I get them developed. I usually can't remember what all the peculiar

STEP TWO   I next paint in the sky, though in this case there was so little sky that it didn't have any great influence on the picture, except to add to the general warm tone of the scene.

spots of light and shade are supposed to represent. The fact that I'm the world's worst photographer may have some bearing on my lack of success when I attempt to work from photographs.

A great many of my friends, on the other hand, seem to get excellent results when they paint from photographs. So I guess it's all right to use photos if you find that they help you to paint a satisfactory picture.

When you're working from a photograph, you can always change things around a little to get a more decorative effect in your painting. It's never necessary to copy the photograph exactly. In fact, your painting will look a lot better if you just concentrate on the important parts and leave out all the unessential details.

FINISHING OUTDOOR PAINTINGS IN THE STUDIO

In addition to the more imaginative and creative painting that you may do in the studio, it's often necessary to add some finishing touches to your outdoor paintings. Very often, you'll want to make some readjust-

STEP THREE   I paint in the general pattern of darks in the composition. As you can see, I used an S-shaped composition in this picture.

ments in color or tone or correct a few minor mistakes. When you are outdoors, working continuously on a painting, your eye becomes tired and it's difficult to see the mistakes. Later in the studio, studying it with a fresh eye, you can make any necessary adjustments.

There's just one thing to remember about working on these outdoor pictures in the studio. Be careful not to overwork them. It's easy to spoil a fresh, spirited sketch by making too many corrections. So just work on the more obvious mistakes and leave the rest alone. When you start to correct a picture, it's very easy to make so many changes that you lose the whole original effect; you can end up with an entirely different picture.

If you're dissatisfied with your rendition of a scene, but you still think that it has good pictorial possibilities, it's much better to take a fresh canvas and paint a new version of the same picture. In this way, you

STEP FOUR   I painted the different parts of the dark pattern in their proper values, especially the dark fir trees and their reflection in the stream. I also painted the light areas in their proper values, with careful attention to the shadows on the snow and the frozen ice along the edge of the stream.

VERMONT STREAM   This is the completed picture, with more detail added. The light striking the facing snow bank in the center of the picture draws attention to the center of interest; namely, the bare trees and evergreens on the point in the middle of the picture. This painting was done from a careful pencil sketch made on the spot. I also made notes on the sketch naming approximate color of the different areas.

still have your original painting in case your second effort doesn't work out as well as you'd hoped.

A painting can be good even if it isn't a perfect picture. You'll often find that some of the sloppy touches add to the effectiveness of the whole composition. To me, a picture that looks just a little bit unfinished is much more interesting than a painting that has been completely polished up in the studio. In other words, always leave something to the imagination.

You probably remember the old saying that it takes two people to paint a masterpiece: one to paint the picture, the other one to hit him over the head with a hammer just before the artist starts to spoil it. I'm very fortunate to have a willing expert with the hammer in my own home. My Gentle Wife watches me like a hawk to see that I don't over-work any of my own unfinished pictures. As a result, I hardly ever have the opportunity to put in those last, finishing touches that give all artists so much pleasure and do so much damage to the picture.

There are a lot of other ways to ruin a promising picture, but I don't think it'll do us any good to dwell on all the unpleasant mistakes an artist can make. I believe that it's better to try to look on the bright side of every problem and remember only the successes, not the failures. I like the idea expressed in the lines engraved on my sundial: "I record only the shining hours."

JOURNEY'S END This old freighter was painted over in Brooklyn from a sketch I made on the spot. I like the hazy appearance of the New York City sky-line. I used the figures on the wharf to add human interest to the scene. The composition of this picture is founded on the idea of the steel-yard's balance. The large dark mass of the freighter with the figures on the wharf is balanced by the dark note of the barges on the right-hand side of the picture.

148

GRAY DAY I painted this picture of one end of Marsh's Pond on a dark overcast day. Before I could finish, it started to rain, so I had to complete the painting in the studio. As you can see, it is a very simple two-toned pattern of light and dark. The trees, distant hills, and the reflections in the water were all part of the dark pattern, while the sky, its reflection in the water, and the light ground in the lower left-hand corner formed the light pattern. I tried to avoid overworking the picture by adding too many details.

FULTON'S FISH MARKET I thought that the fishing boats at the wharf and the dimly seen silhouette of the city in the background made a fascinating subject for a painting. I made a few pencil notes of the scene and painted the picture later in the studio more or less from memory. I tried to get the feeling and atmosphere of the scene rather than a factual or literal copy of it. Courtesy, The Kennedy Galleries.

13. Creative Painting

Fortunately, an artist isn't a camera. He doesn't have to make an exact copy of a particular scene. After he's learned how to use the tools of his trade and can paint a scene the way it really looks, then he can use artistic license if he wishes. He can paint with more imagination and less attention to absolute realism.

When we speak of creative painting today, we immediately think of modern painting: abstract, semi-abstract, or abstract-expressionist. These types of painting are creative and imaginative; but in this book I don't think we need concern ourselves with this kind of painting. I'd rather mention a few ideas that may help you to add a more unusual, more imaginative look to a conventional landscape.

The kind of a picture that I like best is basically realistic in concept, but features some special mood, light effect, or arbitrary color scheme. A very commonplace scene can often be transformed into a fascinating picture by the use of a little imagination and inventiveness on the part of the artist.

CREATIVE USE OF ATMOSPHERE

Atmospheric effect can add a great deal to the success of a picture. A landscape that lacks interest, when viewed in the middle of the day, will often look much more striking if you try painting it in fog. Or you might use the long shadows of late afternoon, with sunlight dramatizing a specific area for greater interest. Perhaps you can use a dark, dramatic sky, making the painting into a storm scene. Then again, you might silhouette the main area against the setting sun.

There are certainly any number of moods in nature to choose from. Over the years, your outdoor painting will enable you to portray the various moods in a convincing manner.

AFTERMATH   This wreckage left along the Jersey coast by one of the big storms was of course painted in the studio. I listened to a news report on the radio one evening and was fascinated by the account of the destruction along the shore. This is the way I thought it might look after the storm was over. I added the two figures to suggest the feeling of loss and desolation which they must have felt when they saw the wreckage of their home.

THE RETURN   I saw this old abandoned shack on the way up the California coast from San Diego to Laguna Beach. The picture is painted in a very simple color scheme: browns, a few grays, and yellow. I decided to paint the scene at the end of the day, with the figure and old shack silhouetted against a bright yellow sky. I added the figure of the old man to give a touch of human interest to the scene. This is a composition with a dark base and a light upper part. Collection, Mr. and Mrs. Frederick F. Fuessenich.

IMAGINATIVE COLOR

Another way to give a more imaginative effect to a picture is to change its color scheme.

Nature has a habit of including a great many colors in the same scene. This lavish display of color is often very confusing. Even when you're painting outdoors, it's a good plan to include only the *three* most important colors of the scene in your painting. By using a very limited color scheme—perhaps one predominating color and a small amount of its complementary for accents—you can often produce a simple, but striking harmony that bears very little resemblance to the more commonplace colors of the original scene.

There are very few scenes that would not be improved if they were painted in a limited color scheme. Two or three analogous colors are often all that you need to produce a pleasing and harmonious picture. Remember, a picture with comparatively few colors has more quality and distinction than a painting that makes use of every color in the rainbow.

FREE BRUSHWORK

A loose, almost sketchy style of painting is much more pleasant than careful, laborious brushwork. A picture should always look as though it were fun to paint, never as though it were drudgery. Just try to suggest the drawing of objects in your picture, rather than whittling them out. You'll find that you can leave many portions of your painting almost unfinished and they will look perfectly all right.

If there are a few parts of the picture that the viewer won't quite understand at first glance, don't worry about them. A certain amount of mystery in a painting only adds to its interest. I'm sure that a painting which requires a little study is much more interesting to the viewer than one in which the entire meaning is obvious at a glance. This is why night scenes and fog effects are so fascinating to almost everyone. All the soft, lost edges produce an air of unreality and mystery, which is a pleasant contrast to our modern, commonplace world.

EXPERIMENTATION

I think an artist needs to do a great deal of experimenting in order to grow artistically. You can't just stand still and try to repeat your former

PUNALUU, OAHU   The northern shore of Oahu, in the Hawaiian Islands, has a much heavier rainfall than other parts of the island. I painted this scene between showers when some of the clouds were below the mountain tops. While Honolulu and Waikiki are pretty much over-run by tourists, it is still possible to find spots on the island which are entirely unspoiled. We loved the Hawaiian Isands, but I found them almost too beautiful to paint. Collection, Mr. J. Brewster Rice.

THE BLACK MESA This painting was done from a sketch that I made on the spot in New Mexico. I used a very simple analogous color scheme of brown, tan, and a warm green. I tried to paint the picture with as little detail as possible, to give a broad impression of the scene.

triumphs. An artist needs new impressions and ideas to keep up his interest in his own work.

You can never tell where you'll find fresh sources of inspiration. It might be some striking atmospheric effect that you see when you're on a jaunt in the country. Or it might be a picture in some gallery, revealing an unusual color scheme or technique. Anything is valuable if it stimulates your imagination and gives you some new ideas to use in your own painting.

There is one great thing about art: all the ideas about color harmonies, design, and painting techniques which have been discovered over the ages are public property. You have just as much right to use them as anyone else. It's all free, so just help yourself.

DISCOVERING FRESH TECHNIQUES

It's fun and often very helpful to experiment with different methods of painting. Painting on a toned canvas can be very interesting. When you're painting a landscape with quite a bit of green in it, a warm, pinkish tone on the canvas makes a very effective contrast to the green areas. A toned canvas is often a help in planning the color scheme for your picture. The single color over the whole canvas gives the effect of a one color harmony; this makes it quite easy to select the other harmonizing or contrasting colors that you need for your painting.

THE EAST RIVER   The East River is more interesting to paint than the Hudson, as it is narrower and has more fascinating bridges to paint. This was a warm picture, with the golden glow of the sky reflected in the water under the bridge. Courtesy, The Kennedy Galleries.

14. Practice Subjects

Sometimes it's interesting to try painting with a palette knife. It certainly helps you to loosen up your work, and it's fun to put on gobs of pure color, mixing them on the canvas. A palette knife painting can have great brilliance and vitality. When a palette knife painting is hung in an exhibition, it tends to make all the other pictures which were painted with a brush look slightly anemic. A few palette knife touches make effective accents in a picture which has been painted with a brush.

You may even find it rewarding to experiment with layers of underpainting covered with semi-transparent glazes of color in the style of a bygone period.

Oriental art has a great deal of charm, with its flat, decorative treatment of color and tone, and its beautiful handling of line. A landscape handled in this manner is extremely decorative and is a pleasant change from the usual, realistic method of painting.

EXPERIMENTAL PALETTES

Though most of my painting is done with the Ballinger palette, I occasionally try painting with other colors, just to see how they work in some of the limited color schemes that I find so interesting. I recently painted several pictures using only burnt sienna, viridian, ivory black, and, of course, zinc white. It was surprising what an interesting effect one could get with this weird assortment of colors. For strictly realistic painting, this choice of colors is not recommended; but for a painting in an arbitrary color scheme, this color selection is very effective. A picture with variations of one strong color, plus ivory black and zinc white, has interesting possibilities.

My Gentle Wife is something of a dual personality. In addition to being my best friend and severest critic, she is also a distinguished portrait painter, known in art circles as Kay Mollison. Though she uses the Ballinger palette for a number of her paintings, she also has a few pet colors of her own that she finds helpful in her figure work. She likes yellow ochre, which is a handsome dull yellow and can be used very effectively. Terra rosa, when combined with cerulean blue, makes lovely grays. Sometimes, for a strong dark, she will use burnt umber—which is a dark, chocolate-like brown—combined with a little ultramarine blue deep.

The only trouble with using earth colors is that they dry so much faster than the cadmiums; the earth colors are liable to look gray and lifeless, while the other colors are still wet and brilliant. However, if you spray

PRACTICE SUBJECT I   In this first practice subject, we have a winter landscape. You could paint the bare trees, bushes, and distant hill in tones of reddish brown, using this also for parts of the stream. The sky could be a pale pink; the evergreens and their reflections in the water a warm green; the shadows cast by the trees a pale blue; the ice along the shore of the creek a delicate green-gray. The snow on the facing bank of the stream would be the lightest part of the picture and would have a creamy white.

the earth colors with a little retouching varnish, their original depth of color will be restored. If you like to paint with earth colors, it would probably be wiser to use them exclusively and not try to mix them with other, more brilliant colors.

OIL PAINT ON PAPER

There is one other way of painting that I almost forgot to mention: painting in oils on paper. It works like a charm and you can get a pleasant

PRACTICE SUBJECT II   This is a sunset scene with a brilliant sky reflected in the still water of a winding stream. You could refer to the picture of the Essex Marshes (page 133) for a possible color scheme. The stream would reflect the color of the sky above it, and would be part of the light pattern. The parts of the clouds in shadow, the hills, trees, and marsh grass along the river would all be part of the dark pattern. This should be a warm picture.

effect very easily, since the paper absorbs a little of the paint. You can go over the same areas a moment later with different color or value, and the effect is about the same as painting over dry color.

If you use watercolor paper of a medium roughness, you'll be able to get some interesting dry-brush effects. Oil on paper works just about like opaque watercolor. For many of the sketches and diagrams in this book, I have used oils on paper.

PRACTICE SUBJECT III   This is an autumn scene. You can refer to the frontispiece to help you select the color scheme of your picture. The trees with darker foliage could be painted in rich dark reds. The light trees in the middle distance and the sparse foliage of the trees at the right side of the picture could be in warm yellow. The distant hills are blue-gray; the field a tannish green, with a few warm grays in the stone wall and on the trunks and branches of some of the trees. You could use a dark greenish brown on some of the tree-trunks and shadows along the wall. The sky could be a light warm gray.

We find that life in New England in the winter time is a bit rugged. Generally, along about January or February, we feel like heading for a warmer, more pleasant climate. In the course of our wanderings, we've spent considerable time on the Pacific coast, and in Mexico, Hawaii, and the Caribbean.

However, it's not necessary to leave the United States to find interest-

PRACTICE SUBJECT IV   This rainy day scene can be painted in a rather cool color scheme. You could use a fairly cool green in the grass, the foliage of the foreground trees, and the roof of the church. The distant trees could be more of a blue-gray than a green. You can also use a little blue-gray in the sky to suggest a rainy day. The church and the other white houses could be in tones of tan and green-gray. The reflections of the trees and figures could be a grayish-brown, as well as the trunks and branches of the trees. The figures would be suggested as dark silhouettes, with perhaps a red coat on the girl in the foreground. You can use a trace of warmth in the lighter parts of the sky and its reflections in the road and sidewalks.

ing subjects to paint. In this country, we have some of the most inspiring scenery in the world. In this book, I'm including pictures that were painted in some of my favorite localities throughout the country.

In this chapter, I've prepared outline drawings of ten different kinds of landscape which you can use as material for some practice paintings of your own. These are only ideas for pictures and have not been painted before. So any picture that you do from these drawings will not be a

PRACTICE SUBJECT V   This is a picture with a sky occupying almost two-thirds of the picture. You could study the color reproduction of *The Road to Harwinton* (page 80) for some ideas to use in the color scheme for this picture. The distant hills could be a blue-gray. The barns and the foliage of the dark trees could be a purplish brown; the fields tan and warm gray-green; the fine branches at the tops of the trees also purplish brown. The dark pattern in the sky would be the blue pattern of the sky behind the light clouds. You could have the top edge of the clouds a little lighter, with a suggestion of shadow on the lower areas. The roof of the house could be a light tan and the barn roof reflecting the color of the sky.

copy of someone else's finished work, but I hope they will be more of your own creation.

I'll suggest a possible treatment for each picture, but you'll probably want to try out your own ideas on some of the sketches. You'll find that you can produce a number of different pictures from each sketch, simply by changing the color scheme, the light effect, or the over-all mood of the entire painting.

PRACTICE SUBJECT VI   For this spring landscape you could more or less use the color scheme of *Spring on Cotton Hill* (page 115). The new leaves on the trees in the center of the picture would be in shades of pale green, as would the trees across the meadow on the left. The evergreens are a warm dark green. The distant hills are a purplish brown, with a little blue-gray added in the last line of hills. The weeds and bushes would be in tones of orange-brown. The stone wall and some of the trunks and branches of the trees would be a warm gray; the sky a pale pink near the tops of the hills, with the upper clouds a darker gray.

It's quite possible that you may get on to some more original ways of completing these sketches than the ways that I'll suggest. I hope that you'll try to work out your own ideas. There's nothing that would please me more than to know that you're using your imagination and creative ability to paint an original picture of your own.

PRACTICE SUBJECT VII   I made this sketch of some farm buildings near Aspen, Colorado. You might look at the Georgetown, Colorado illustration (page 67) for an idea of the color of that region. The aspen trees on the mountain-side in the center of the picture were a golden yellow, as were the trees and bushes in the lower right-hand corner. The light fields were a mixture of tan and greenish yellow; the barns and field on the right a purplish brown; the evergreen trees a warm dark green. The hills were a brownish purple, with a little gray-green. The distant snow-capped peaks were blue, with cool shadows in the snow. The sky was a pinkish blue.

PRACTICE SUBJECT VIII   This is another view of *Rockport's Motif No. 1* in a fog. If you study the reproduction of *The Motif* (page 137), you will have an idea of the color you might like to use. The old fish-house would be a rather faded pink when seen through the fog; the stone wharf a mixture of tan and gray-green; the distant boat a grayish tan. The man's trousers and the boat with the outboard motor could be a dark greenish brown; the other two boats green, with some brown and green reflected in the water. The sky would be a little lighter and warmer around the top of the fish-house, and also on the water to the left of the figure in the boat. Sometimes you can paint the fog with a little warmth running through it. At least be sure that the fog isn't all a cold gray. The boat at the dock would be a combination of pale tan and faint warm green.

PRACTICE SUBJECT IX   This is a moonlight scene. The light from the moon, which is just out of the picture, falls on the tops of the clouds. The darker portions of the sky could be a blue-green. The barns, house, the ground, and reflections in the pond could be painted with a combination of dark blue and brown. The light on the clouds, the roof of the barn, and the light part of the pond would be a cool gray with just a little pale yellow to suggest the feeble warmth of the moon. You could use a touch of a warmer yellow in the lighted windows of the house.

PRACTICE SUBJECT X   In this snow scene, the barns, the roof of the house, and distant hills could be a reddish brown. The house and the long grass poking through the snow in the foreground can be painted a golden tan. Small branches at the tops of the trees are a purple-brown. The sky is a pale pinkish gray. The stone wall is a mixture of gray-green and darker browns. These colors could also be used for the trunks of the trees. Since the light is coming from the right side of the picture, you will see cool shadows to the left of the house and barns and along the stone wall. You might suggest a few warm touches of red in the brush along the wall and the chimney of the house. Be sure to keep a little warmth in the white of the snow.

15. Developing Your Professional Skills

In writing this book, I've tried to cover all the knowledge of landscape painting, and art in general, that I've acquired in my painting career. I've included all of the really important information that I think you'll need in planning and painting your own landscapes.

My instruction has been confined to the practical side—the mechanics of picture-making—rather than a discussion of art esthetics and abstract principles, which sound very impressive but are not necessarily any help in painting a good picture.

The important steps in painting a landscape have been described in the kind of language I can understand myself: in words of one syllable. I've tried to avoid making a mystery of the steps necessary to produce a picture. The principles and ideas that I've explained are the ones I've used in all my own pictures, as you can see from the illustrations in this book.

GROWING TOWARD PROFESSIONAL WORK

Unfortunately, you cannot become a good artist merely by reading a book on painting. It'll take a lot of hard work and study to learn to paint a fine picture. However, it's fun to sketch and paint; you can enjoy yourself at any level of proficiency while you're learning. Of course, you'll take more pleasure in your work as you learn to paint a better picture.

I suspect that this book—which was intended to contain just the fundamentals of picture-making for the beginner or amateur painter—has developed into a book for the serious student and the professional artist. As I wrote, I couldn't resist putting in all the ideas I thought might help you to create a more professionally painted picture. In other words, I don't want my readers to *remain* on an amateur level. I want them to paint first-class pictures in an entirely professional manner. I can't see any reason why, one of these days, you can't paint some excellent pictures of your own. In fact, I'll be very much disappointed if your own work doesn't show a steady improvement as time passes.

THE LONG ROAD When I painted this picture, I wanted to suggest our long rough road through life. But when I looked at the painting I thought it might just as well represent the long road to artistic achievement. My Gentle Wife dislikes ghostly figures in pictures and generally makes some disparaging remarks about them. However, when I am painting a symbolic picture like this, I always carefully explain to her that the hooded figure is not a Ku Klux Klansman and that I do not consider it a morbid touch in the painting, but rather a note of dramatic interest. So I occasionally enjoy painting a picture like this, in spite of the loud protests from my Best Friend and Severest Critic.

171

DEVELOPING ORIGINALITY

I've often been asked how a student could work out an original technique of his own.

I wouldn't advise copying a painting by another artist. When you're copying a picture, you don't have to use your imagination or do any thinking. Consequently, you're not learning as much as you would if you were working on an original picture of your own. However, as the practice subjects in Chapter 14 were merely sketches and never intended as finished pictures, I think it will be all right to use them to work out some of your own ideas.

If you study the work of a number of other artists and don't try to imitate any one painter's style, you'll find that your work won't be a copy of any particular artist's work; your own work will look entirely original. Everyone instinctively has a way of painting that is easiest and most natural for him. This is your own style. With practice, certain painting habits and mannerisms will begin to show up in your work, giving it an entirely personal and original appearance. In other words, just do what comes naturally.

THE ELEMENTS OF A SUCCESSFUL PICTURE

If you'll forgive the repetition, I'd like to summarize briefly the three important elements of a successful picture. They are good drawing, good composition, and good color.

As drawing is the foundation of every picture, be sure that everything in the picture has been well drawn, in the right proportions to the other objects in the picture. Whether you're drawing with a pencil or a brush, you're constantly drawing when you're painting a picture. So don't get so preoccupied with slopping paint around that you forget to draw correctly.

If you carry a sketchbook around with you and form the habit of sketching everything that interests you, you'll find that this habit helps your drawing and gives you a lot of good reference material for your pictures.

After all my talk about trying to work out a pleasing and decorative composition, I know that you won't forget this important framework of a picture. Whenever you're outdoors and see an interesting scene, try to figure out its basic design. At an exhibition, make a note of the pattern of any picture that appeals to you.

Your color sense will improve with practice and you'll be able to get more pleasing harmonies in your paintings. You'll discover that the simplest color schemes are sometimes the best. You'll learn to avoid too complicated a choice of colors. And you'll also learn what colors look well together and you'll be able to combine them with good taste.

Outdoor painting is just as important to an artist as grammar is to a writer. I hope that you'll try to paint from nature on every possible occasion. When you get so old and feeble that you can't get around outdoors any more, that'll be the day to start doing all your work in the studio.

Painting a landscape isn't so difficult; it's only when you try to paint a *good* one that you're liable to run into trouble.

After this profound thought, may I say in closing that I'd like to wish all the readers of this book the best of luck, and all possible success, in painting landscapes.

THE BAIT-DIGGERS   This picture was painted at East Gloucester just before dark. The soft light from the sky gave the picture a romantic and mysterious quality which I found fascinating to paint.

Index

Edited by Donald Holden

Designed by William Harris

Photographs of paintings by Irving Blomstrann

Composed in Twelve Point Baskerville by Atlantic Linotype Company, Inc.

Engravings by Pioneer Moss, Inc.

Offset by Affiliated Lithographers, Inc.

Four-color letterpress by Van Rees Press

Bound by Chas. H. Bohn Company, Inc.